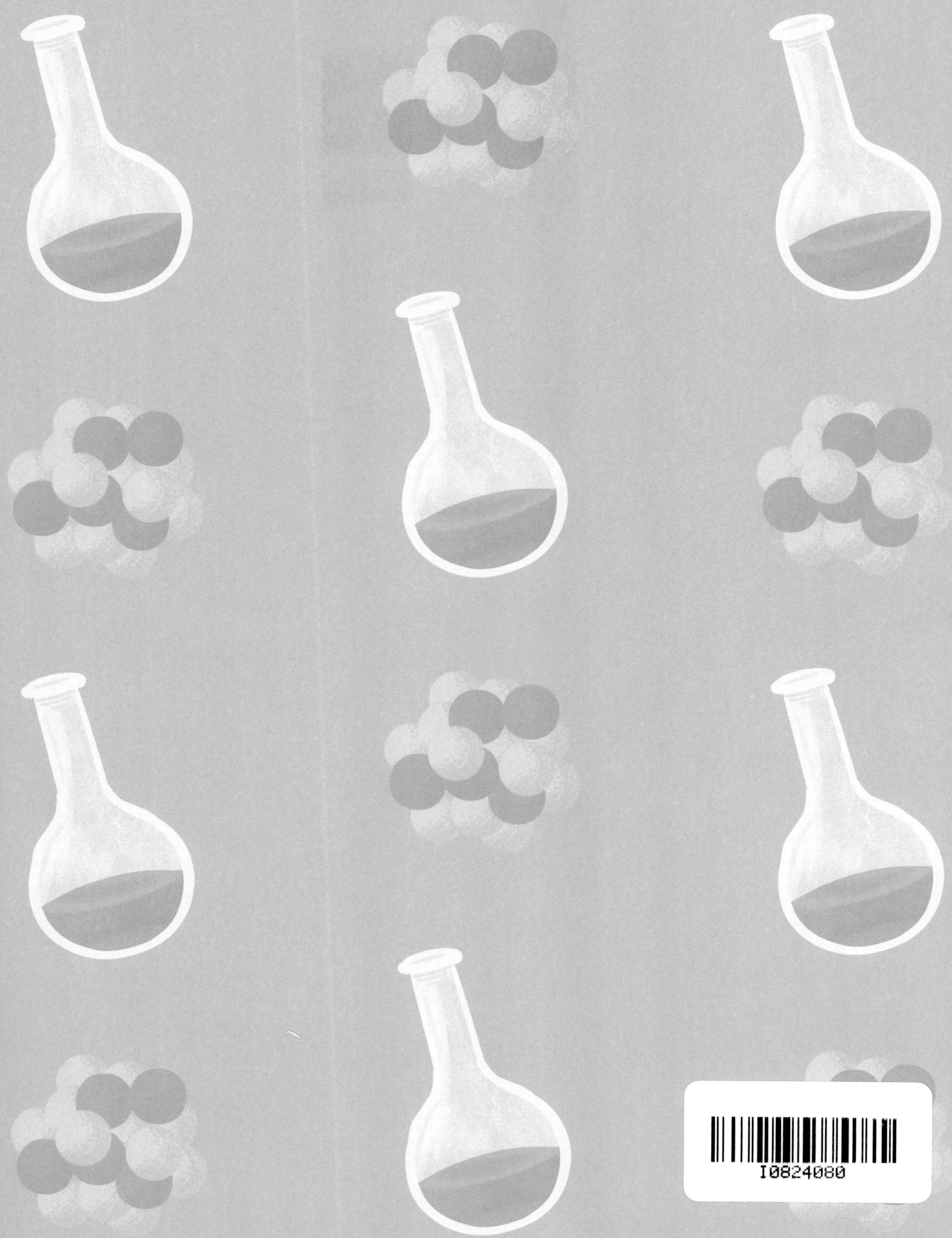

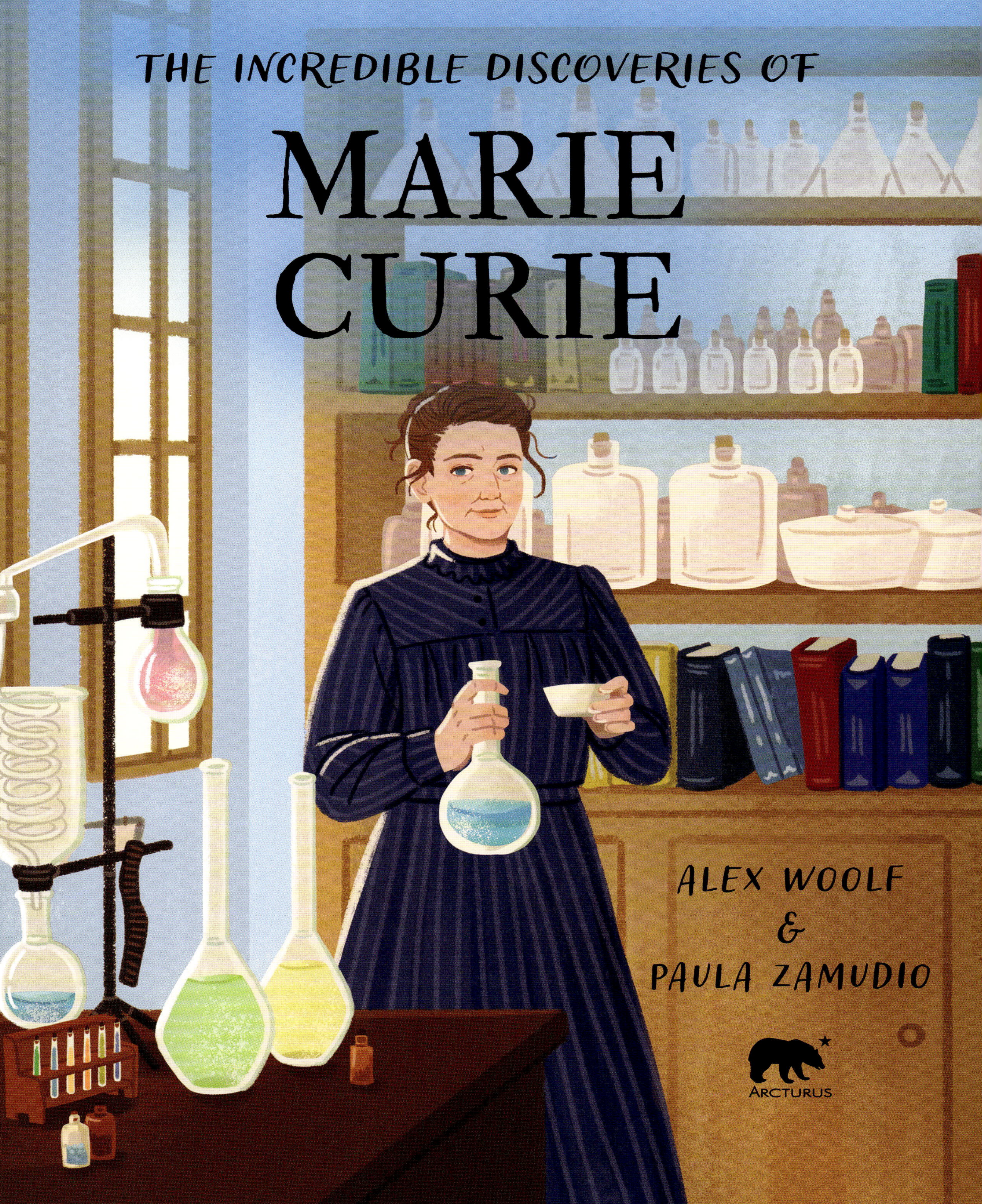
THE INCREDIBLE DISCOVERIES OF
MARIE
CURIE
ALEX WOOLF
&
PAULA ZAMUDIO
ARCTURUS

ARCTURUS

This edition published in 2026 by Arcturus Publishing Limited
26/27 Bickels Yard, 151–153 Bermondsey Street,
London SE1 3HA

Writer: Alex Woolf
Illustrator: Paula Zamudio
Designer: Ariadne Ward
Consultant: Anna Claybourne
Editors: Lydia Halliday and Rebecca Razo
Managing Editor: Becca Clunes
Managing Designer: Georgina Wood
Development Director: Joe Harris

ISBN: 978-1-3988-6921-9
CH012456NT
Supplier 29, Date 1225, PI 00012202

Printed in China

CONTENTS

INTRODUCTION

A REVOLUTIONARY SCIENTIST

Marie Curie was a remarkable scientist whose discoveries helped unravel the mysteries of radioactivity and broke new ground in physics and chemistry. As the first woman to win a Nobel Prize—and the first person to win two Nobel prizes—she blazed a trail for women in science.

Atoms

Marie Curie devoted her life to the study of radioactivity. To understand what that is, we need to understand atoms. Atoms are the tiny units that make up all matter. Everything around us, from houses to cars and people to animals, is made of atoms. Atoms consist of three kinds of particles—protons, neutrons and electrons. Protons and neutrons are in the middle (nucleus) of the atom. Electrons circle around the nucleus.

Isotopes

The number of protons in every atom reveals its chemical makeup, or element. Carbon, for example, always has 6 protons, whereas chlorine always has 17. However, atoms can have different numbers of neutrons and still be the same element. Atoms of the same element with different numbers of neutrons are called isotopes. The isotope carbon-14, for example, has 6 protons and 8 neutrons, whereas carbon-12 has 6 protons and 6 neutrons.

Radioactivity

If the nucleus of an isotope has too many, or too few, neutrons, it becomes unstable and releases energy in the form of a particle so it can return to a more stable state. This process is known as radioactive decay. The energy released when a nucleus releases a particle is called radioactivity.

Types of radioactivity

If a nucleus contains too few neutrons, it emits an alpha particle (2 protons and 2 neutrons bound together). If there are too many neutrons, it emits a beta particle (an electron), which changes a neutron into a proton. These changes in the nucleus can leave it in an "excited" or "hot" state, so the nucleus emits a type of energy called a gamma ray to cool it down. In rare cases, a nucleus may emit a single neutron or proton.

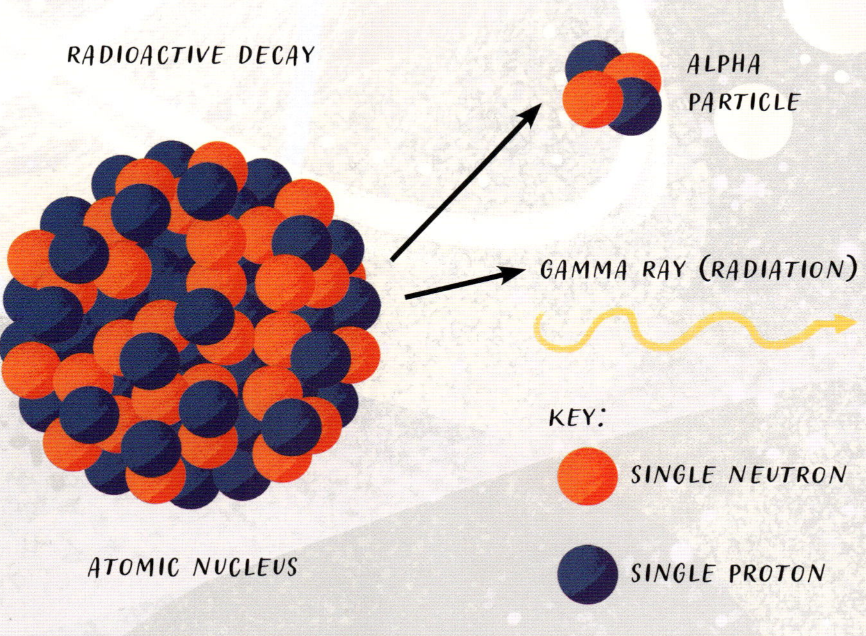

Understanding radioactivity

Radioactivity has existed in nature since the beginning of the Universe. But it wasn't discovered by humans until the 1890s. Marie Curie began the process of understanding what radioactivity is, laying the foundations for great innovations in science, technology, and medicine.

RESISTING GENDER NORMS

When Marie Curie was growing up in the 19th century, women were not expected to become scientists. Their education was designed to prepare them for life as a wife and mother, so they studied subjects such as music, needlework, and home-making. There was little opportunity for them to study subjects like science; however, Marie Curie refused to let society's standards prevent her from reaching her goals.

Getting an education

In Poland, where Marie grew up, women weren't allowed to attend university. So, Marie moved to Paris, France, to get a higher education. Even in France, there were limits on the number of women admitted to the university each year.

THE SORBONNE UNIVERSITY IN PARIS

Social barriers

The women who were admitted to university often struggled to be taken seriously by their male counterparts and professors. At that time, many male scientists didn't believe women could achieve great things in science.

A difficult balance

In Marie's day, when men became fathers, it did not disrupt their work, as they weren't expected to carry out childcare duties or manage the home. However, when Marie became a mother, she was fortunate to get a lot of help from Pierre's father, who looked after the children, so that she could continue with her scientific work.

Being excluded

As a young scientist, Marie found it hard to secure money and a laboratory to conduct her experiments. Before she became famous, Marie lacked opportunities to discuss her work with other scientists and benefit from their experience. She simply was not accepted by the scientific establishment. Because of her gender, Marie was twice denied membership to the French Academy of Science. Even after she and her husband made their great discoveries, many assumed she had merely been his assistant.

Marie's achievements

With so many obstacles blocking her way, Marie Curie's scientific achievements are all the more impressive. She succeeded thanks to her intelligence and perseverance. In doing so, she helped blaze a trail for women scientists in the future.

SCIENCE BEFORE CURIE

In the mid-1890s, when Marie Curie was embarking on her career as a scientist, the scientific community had become fascinated by a newly discovered form of radiation known as X-rays.

The history of X-rays

On November 8, 1895, German physicist Wilhelm Roentgen was experimenting in his lab with a cathode-ray tube—a glass tube with no air inside—through which a stream of electrons is fired. Roentgen covered the tube with black paper and fired it at some crystals a short distance away. To his surprise, the crystals produced a green glow. Roentgen had discovered a new kind of invisible ray that could pass through paper. He later found out that these X-rays, as he called them, could also pass through the soft tissues of the body.

Phosphorescent crystals

At this same time, French physicist Henri Becquerel was studying phosphorescence—the glow produced by some substances when they're exposed to light. (Glow-in-the-dark toys and clockfaces use phosphorescence.) Becquerel thought Roentgen's X-rays were related to phosphorescence. To prove it, in 1896 he tried exposing some phosphorescent uranium crystals to the Sun, and then placed them on a photographic plate. When he exposed the plate, he saw a black image of the crystals on it. Becquerel believed the crystals must have emitted X-rays when exposed to the Sun, and that they had blackened the plate.

Radioactivity discovered

Becquerel wanted to test his idea by exposing more crystals to the Sun; however, he was forced to pause the experiment when the weather changed. He put the uranium crystals in a drawer, together with a photographic plate. The next day, he exposed the plate, expecting to see a feeble image. Instead, to his amazement, the plate showed clear, black images of the crystals. This meant the uranium crystals were emitting radiation by themselves without any energy from the Sun. Becquerel had just discovered radioactivity!

Mysteries to uncover

This was the state of the science when Marie Curie first arrived on the scene. Scientists knew about radioactivity, though they didn't yet have a name for it (Curie herself would come up with the name in 1898), and they had no idea what caused it.

CURIE'S LIFE

EARLY LIFE

For the first 24 years of her life, Marie Curie was called Maria Skłodowska. She was born in Warsaw, Poland, on November 7, 1867, the youngest of three sisters and one brother. Both of her parents were schoolteachers and believed in educating their children equally, which was unusual for the time.

Humble beginnings

At this time, Warsaw was part of the Russian Empire. Maria's parents' families campaigned for an independent Poland, which made the Russian authorities angry. As a result, much of the family's wealth and property were confiscated; therefore, Maria's family was quite poor. Sadly, when Maria was seven, her eldest sister Zofia died of typhus; when Maria was ten, her mother died of tuberculosis.

MARIE AS A CHILD AT SCHOOL

Early education

In 1878, Maria began attending a school for girls. Helped by her father, who taught mathematics and physics, she proved to be an exceptional student. She graduated with a gold medal at age 16. Although Maria was not allowed to enroll in college in Poland, she refused to give up on her dreams of becoming a scientist.

The Flying University

Maria and her sister Bronya attended the Flying University (sometimes translated as the Floating University)—a secret, illegal university where women could study. It got its name because they met in private homes around Warsaw, changing location regularly to avoid getting caught.

Tutor and governess

Maria was determined to continue her scientific studies in Paris. But first she would have to raise some money. She found work as a tutor. After that, she worked for two years as a governess for a wealthy family, teaching the children and managing household tasks. Life was not easy, but she stayed focused on her goal.

A new opportunity

While working as a governess, Maria continued her studies in her spare time. She even got to use a chemistry laboratory in Warsaw. In 1891, her sister Bronya, who had already moved to Paris, invited Maria to stay with her. It was the opportunity she had been waiting for.

MARIE WORKING AS A GOVERNESS TO TWO CHILDREN

A LIFE-CHANGING MOVE

In Paris, Maria (or Marie, as she now called herself) lived briefly with her sister before finding her own place to rent. She enrolled at the University of Paris, known as the Sorbonne, where she continued her studies of physics, chemistry, and mathematics.

Fearless determination

Marie studied during the day in her small attic room and worked as a tutor in the evenings. She was poor and lived mainly on bread, butter, and tea. She kept herself warm in winter by wearing all her clothes at the same time.

A big achievement

Marie's hard work was rewarded, and in 1893 she received her degree in physics, achieving the highest marks in her class. She began working in an industrial laboratory, investigating the magnetic properties of different kinds of steel. Meanwhile, she continued her studies at the Sorbonne and was awarded a degree in mathematical sciences in 1894, achieving the second-highest marks in her class.

"It would ... be a beautiful thing to pass through life together hypnotized in our dreams: your dream for your country; our dream for humanity; our dream for science."
Letter from Pierre to Marie

Meeting Pierre Curie

In 1894, Marie met Pierre Curie, who would become the love of her life. Pierre was a teacher of physics, and it was their mutual passion for science that brought them together. Soon they developed feelings for each other, and in July 1895 they got married. As well as working on their science, they both loved long bicycle rides and journeys abroad. In 1897, they had their first child, Irène.

Uranium rays

In 1896, Marie became interested in a recent discovery by Henri Becquerel (see page 8). His experiments showed that uranium crystals emitted rays similar to X-rays that seemed to come from the uranium itself. She thought these uranium rays might be a suitable subject for a thesis (a long essay) for her doctorate (the highest degree awarded by a university). To give her time to prepare her thesis, Pierre's father, a retired doctor, helped look after baby Irène.

NEW DISCOVERIES

In her experiments, Marie worked with a uranium-rich mineral called pitchblende. She discovered that pitchblende was more radioactive than uranium itself. She concluded that the mineral must contain a small quantity of another substance far more radioactive than uranium, and she began a search for this other substance.

Working together

In 1898, Marie discovered that thorium gave off rays in a similar way to uranium, and she published a scientific paper about it. By then, Pierre had become increasingly intrigued by Marie's work and decided to drop his own research and join her. They collaborated as equals, discussing ideas and working as each other's technicians during experiments.

Polonium and radium

In July 1898, the Curies announced their discovery of a new element in a jointly published paper. Marie named it polonium after her home country, which was still under foreign occupation. In December 1898, they announced the existence of another new element, which they named radium.

MARIE AND PIERRE WORKING ON THEIR EXPERIMENTS

The research shed

The Curies set out to isolate radium (separate it from other materials so that it existed in a pure form). This required lots of space, so they moved into a shed, which was damp and poorly ventilated. It took four years to isolate radium chloride, a salt containing radium. At this time, nobody knew the dangers of working with radioactive materials. Marie and Pierre unknowingly exposed themselves to harmful amounts of radiation.

Earning a doctorate

In June 1903, Marie completed her thesis and was awarded a doctorate degree in physics. She was the first woman in France to receive a doctorate. That month, the Curies were invited to the Royal Institution in London to talk about their work on radioactivity; however, because she was a woman, Marie was not allowed to speak. In his speech, Pierre emphasized Marie's vital role in their collaboration.

A new craze

The discovery of radium, with its mysterious glow, caught the public imagination. Soon, a whole industry was launched based on its supposed health benefits. Because the Curies did not patent their discovery, they earned no money from its commercial use. Being poor, they both took teaching jobs to make ends meet. Marie became ill due to her exposure to radiation.

NOBEL PRIZE FOR PHYSICS

In December 1903, the Royal Swedish Academy of Sciences awarded Pierre Curie, Marie Curie, and Henri Becquerel the Nobel Prize in Physics. The prize was awarded in recognition of their collective work on radioactivity. Marie was the first woman to be awarded a Nobel Prize.

Pressure on the Academy

At first, the Academy only intended to reward the two men; however, Pierre defended his wife's work, explaining that it was her research, theories, and experiments that resulted in their discoveries. Under pressure, the Academy added Marie's name to the award. Unfortunately, the Curies could not travel to Sweden to receive the prize in person because they were sick. They felt tired all the time and had burns on their hands from handling radioactive materials. They didn't know it at the time, but they were both suffering from radiation poisoning.

HENRI BECQUEREL RECEIVED THE NOBEL PRIZE IN PERSON, BUT THE CURIES WERE TOO SICK TO ATTEND.

A rise in status

The Nobel Prize transformed the Curies' lives. With the award money they were able to hire their first laboratory assistant, and the Sorbonne gave them their first proper laboratory. As a Nobel Prize winner, Pierre became much in demand. He was offered a position at the University of Geneva, and the Sorbonne offered him a professorship and made him the Chair of Physics. Marie, being a woman, received no such offers. However, Pierre made her the official head of the laboratory.

"I am among those who think that science has great beauty. A scientist in his laboratory is not only a technician: he is also a child placed before natural phenomena which impress him like a fairy tale."
Marie Curie

More than a "helpmate"

Even after winning the Nobel Prize, many male scientists continued to assume that Marie had merely assisted Pierre in his work. At the award ceremony itself, the president of the Swedish Academy described Marie as a "helpmate." It would be many years before her achievements were fully recognized by the scientific community.

A TRAGIC ACCIDENT

On April 19, 1906, tragedy struck. Pierre Curie was rushing through heavy rain in Paris when he stepped in the path of a horse-drawn carriage. He fell under its wheels, fracturing his skull and dying instantly.

A special tribute

Marie wanted to create a state-of-the-art laboratory for the study of radioactivity as a tribute to her husband. The Sorbonne rejected the proposal, so the Pasteur Institute suggested it would build the laboratory instead. When Marie threatened to leave the Sorbonne, the university changed its mind. In 1909, the Sorbonne and the Pasteur Institute jointly established a radioactivity laboratory for Marie. It was named the Curie Pavilion.

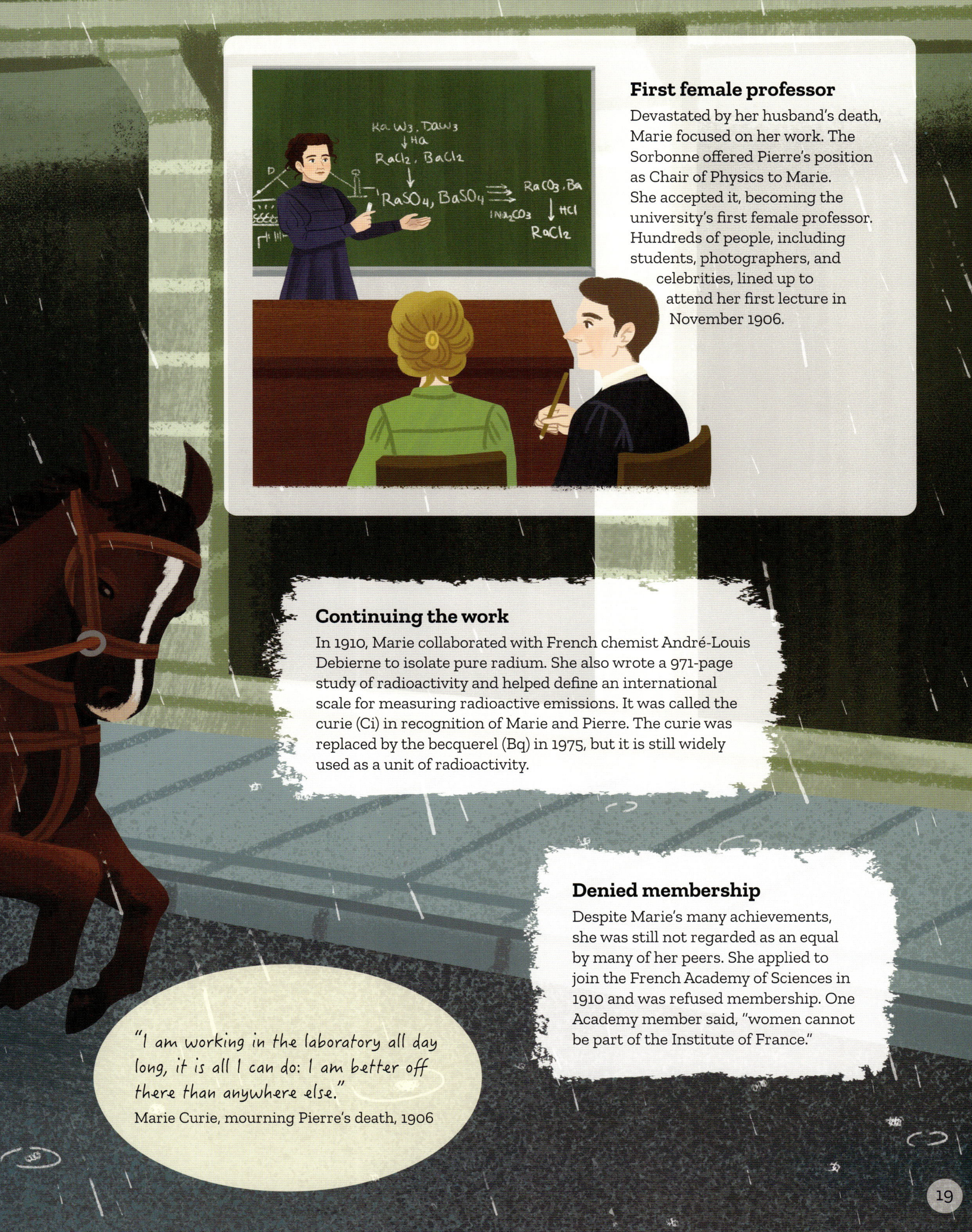

First female professor

Devastated by her husband's death, Marie focused on her work. The Sorbonne offered Pierre's position as Chair of Physics to Marie. She accepted it, becoming the university's first female professor. Hundreds of people, including students, photographers, and celebrities, lined up to attend her first lecture in November 1906.

Continuing the work

In 1910, Marie collaborated with French chemist André-Louis Debierne to isolate pure radium. She also wrote a 971-page study of radioactivity and helped define an international scale for measuring radioactive emissions. It was called the curie (Ci) in recognition of Marie and Pierre. The curie was replaced by the becquerel (Bq) in 1975, but it is still widely used as a unit of radioactivity.

Denied membership

Despite Marie's many achievements, she was still not regarded as an equal by many of her peers. She applied to join the French Academy of Sciences in 1910 and was refused membership. One Academy member said, "women cannot be part of the Institute of France."

"I am working in the laboratory all day long, it is all I can do: I am better off there than anywhere else."
Marie Curie, mourning Pierre's death, 1906

NOBEL PRIZE FOR CHEMISTRY

In November 1911, Marie Curie was awarded the Nobel Prize for Chemistry. This award was for her discovery of polonium and radium, for her isolation of radium, and for her studies of this remarkable element. Marie became the first person ever to receive two Nobel Prizes. She remains the only person, besides Linus Pauling, to win Nobel Prizes in two different fields.

Controversy

Marie's extraordinary achievement was overshadowed by a controversy regarding her private life. In 1911, reports suggested that she was in a relationship with French physicist Paul Langevin, a former student of Pierre's. In those days, gossip like this was damaging and harmed reputations. Marie and Paul refused to comment on the matter. However, due to the controversy, the chair of the Nobel committee tried to stop Marie from attending the award ceremony. Marie pushed back and insisted on attending, saying there was no relation between her scientific work and her private life.

Radium Institute

The second Nobel Prize gave an enormous boost to Marie's reputation. She had managed to overcome much of the gender bias of the time, and her fellow scientists began to regard her with genuine respect. The Warsaw Scientific Society offered Marie the chance to run a new laboratory in Poland, which she set up remotely, but she preferred to remain in France. She persuaded the French government to fund the establishment of new research quarters in Paris. The Radium Institute was to be built on a new street named Rue Pierre-et-Marie-Curie. Here, a large team of scientists would dedicate themselves to the study of radioactivity and its uses. The Radium Institute opened in 1914.

Illness and recovery

A month after accepting her Nobel Prize, Marie became seriously ill with a kidney ailment and had to have an operation. She spent most of 1912 recuperating, only returning to her laboratory in December. In 1913, she began making public appearances again. In March of that year, the famous physicist Albert Einstein paid her a visit. They had met before and became good friends.

WORLD WAR I

In July 1914, war broke out between the major powers of Europe. The Great War, later named World War I, would last for over four years and fighting would spread to many other parts of the world. In France, the front line quickly became deadlocked as soldiers fired at each other from long lines of trenches. There were many casualties, and Marie wanted to help the wounded soldiers.

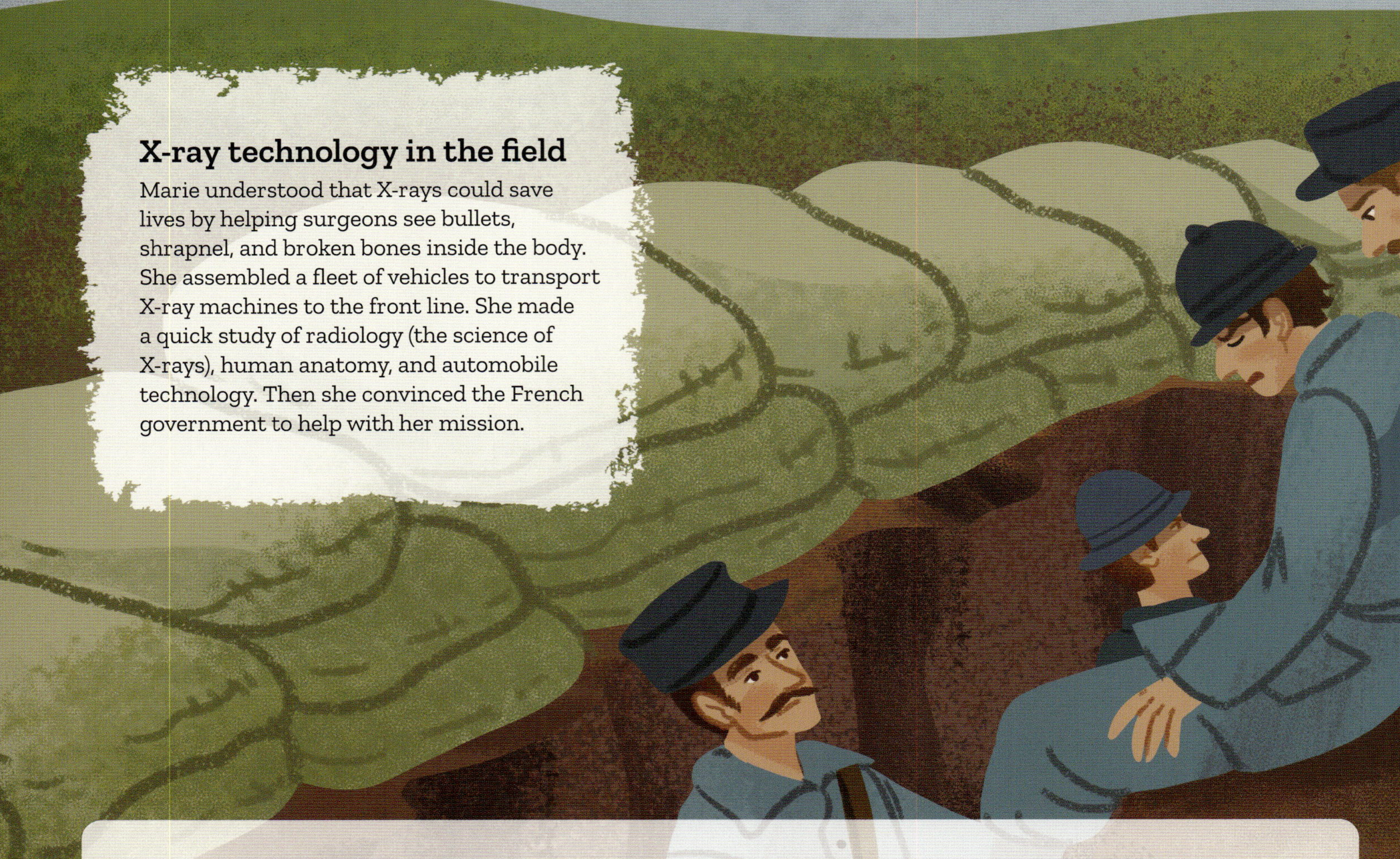

X-ray technology in the field

Marie understood that X-rays could save lives by helping surgeons see bullets, shrapnel, and broken bones inside the body. She assembled a fleet of vehicles to transport X-ray machines to the front line. She made a quick study of radiology (the science of X-rays), human anatomy, and automobile technology. Then she convinced the French government to help with her mission.

Petites Curies

Marie was appointed director of the newly established Red Cross Radiology Service. She acquired donated vehicles and and found mechanics to convert them into trucks. She then coaxed manufacturers to donate X-ray equipment. Marie even learned to drive the trucks herself. By October 1914, the first of twenty radiology vehicles was ready. French soldiers nicknamed them *petites Curies* ("little Curies"). Another 200 radiological units were set up at field hospitals in the first year of the war. It is estimated that, by the end of the war, more than a million soldiers were treated with the help of the radiology units.

X-ray training

Curie supervised training in radiography (the process of producing medical X-rays) for around 1,400 doctors and technicians. She chose her daughter Irène, now 17, as her assistant. Mother and daughter made their first visit to the front line in October 1914. Irène continued to work as a nurse radiographer throughout the war and received a military medal for her contribution. Marie did not receive a medal for her efforts, even though her radiology service saved countless soldiers' lives.

A VISIT TO THE UNITED STATES

MARIE MELONEY INTERVIEWING MARIE CURIE

In 1920, a New York City journalist named Marie "Missy" Meloney interviewed Marie Curie in Paris for the women's magazine, the *Delineator*. This interview would spark a campaign that would ultimately bring Curie to the United States and turn her into a worldwide celebrity.

A gram of radium

In the course of the interview, Meloney learned that Marie had never patented the process for purifying radium, and therefore earned no money from the radium products on the market. Chemical companies were processing radium and selling it for health treatments and military research for $100,000 per gram, but Marie could not afford the element she had discovered. Her Radium Institute currently had a single gram of radium, and her greatest wish was for a second gram.

Campaign for Curie

Eager to help, Meloney created the Marie Curie Radium Fund to raise money to purchase a gram of radium, so Marie could continue her research. Led by a committee of wealthy American women and distinguished scientists, the campaign was a big success. Within months, it had raised more than $100,000. Meloney invited Marie to the United States to be presented with the gift. Embarrassed not to have given Marie more recognition in the past, the French government offered her the highest merit in France for military and civil achievements. However, Marie refused to accept it, due to her former rejection from the French Academy of Sciences earlier in her career.

Coming to America

Marie sailed from France with Irène, 23, and Eve, 16, arriving in New York on May 11, 1921. During the nearly seven-week tour, the Curies were invited to appear at numerous events and functions. Marie was awarded honorary degrees by numerous universities. She made a lot of speeches and shook many hands. The highlight of the tour was a ceremony at the White House in Washington, D.C., where President Warren Harding handed Marie the gram of radium.

AN AMBASSADOR FOR SCIENCE

During the 1920s, Marie Curie did much to advocate for science and raise money for scientific research and education. Despite decades of teaching, Marie suffered from a lifelong fear of public speaking. Yet demand was high for the legendary scientist, and she continued to make public appearances and give lectures despite her nervousness.

"Curie, who handles daily a particle of radium more dangerous than lightning, was afraid when confronted by the necessity of appearing before the public."

Stephane Lauzanne, editor-in-chief of *Le Matin*

Writing books

Marie wanted to broaden public understanding of science, and in 1923 she wrote a book aimed at non-scientists, to teach them about her research into radium. The book, entitled ***Pierre Curie,*** was the biography of her late husband. In it she captured the heroism of scientific research, describing how she and Pierre had to overcome poverty and the hostility of the French scientific establishment to make their discoveries.

Radium Institute

In 1920, Marie, along with her colleagues, created the Curie Foundation. Its mission was to help raise funds for the Radium Institute's research into the treatment of cancer. In 1925, on a visit to Poland, Marie founded a second Radium Institute in Warsaw. Her sister Bronya was appointed its director. To help raise funds for the Warsaw Institute, Marie agreed to go on a second tour of the United States, again organized by Missy Meloney. During this trip, she met President Herbert Hoover.

International work

In August 1922, Marie became a member of the International Committee on Intellectual Cooperation, set up to promote the exchange of ideas between scientists, artists, and intellectuals around the world. Among her fellow members was her friend Albert Einstein. Marie worked toward creating an international bibliography (list of books) of scientific papers and protecting scientists' ownership of rights for their discoveries. In 1930, she was elected to the International Atomic Weights Committee, which helped determine the atomic weights of the elements. She saw these jobs as important, but still missed the joy of doing scientific work in the laboratory.

LATER YEARS

In 1920, Marie had cataracts in both eyes (this is where the lens of the eye becomes clouded). Today, we know this was caused by exposure to radiation. Her vision became so poor that she had to write her lecture notes in giant letters and ask her daughters to guide her around. She required four operations to correct her eyesight.

Dangers of radiation

Marie had suffered frequent medical problems since she began working with radioactive substances. At the time, the dangers of exposure to radiation were largely unknown. Throughout the 1920s, most people believed that low levels of radiation had health benefits. By the time doctors realized the dangers, it was too late for Marie.

Declining health

During the early 1930s, Marie's decades of work with radium and other substances caught up with her, and she became very sick. On days when she was too ill to make it to the laboratory, she would work on her new book, *Radioactivity*, which would be published after her death.

Irène and Eve

Marie lived long enough to see her daughters achieve success in their chosen fields. Irène became a scientist at the Radium Institute. In an echo of her mother's life, she married another researcher, Frédéric Joliot, and collaborated with him in her research. The Joliot-Curies discovered artificial radioactivity, for which they won the Nobel Prize for Chemistry in 1935. Marie's other daughter, Eve, became a journalist and musician. In 1937, she wrote a best-selling biography of her mother.

IN 1937, EVE CURIE WROTE A BEST-SELLING BIOGRAPHY OF HER MOTHER.

Death

In April 1934, Marie visited Poland to see her family. It proved to be a farewell visit. On July 4, she died, aged 66, from aplastic anemia, a disease of the bone marrow, which was caused by long-term radiation poisoning.

Burial

Marie was buried alongside her husband in the cemetery at Sceaux, south of Paris. In 1995, the bodies of Marie and Pierre were transferred to the Panthéon in Paris, where the most celebrated French citizens are buried. Marie Curie was only the second woman to be interred there.

CURIE'S DISCOVERIES

THE ATOM IS DIVISIBLE

The excitement about Henri Becquerel's 1896 discovery of uranium rays quickly faded. They didn't seem as useful as X-rays, being too weak to produce good images of bones. Also, minerals containing uranium weren't easy to access—unlike X-rays, which could be produced with a special glass tube and electricity. If Marie Curie hadn't written about Becquerel's rays in her doctoral thesis, they might have been forgotten altogether.

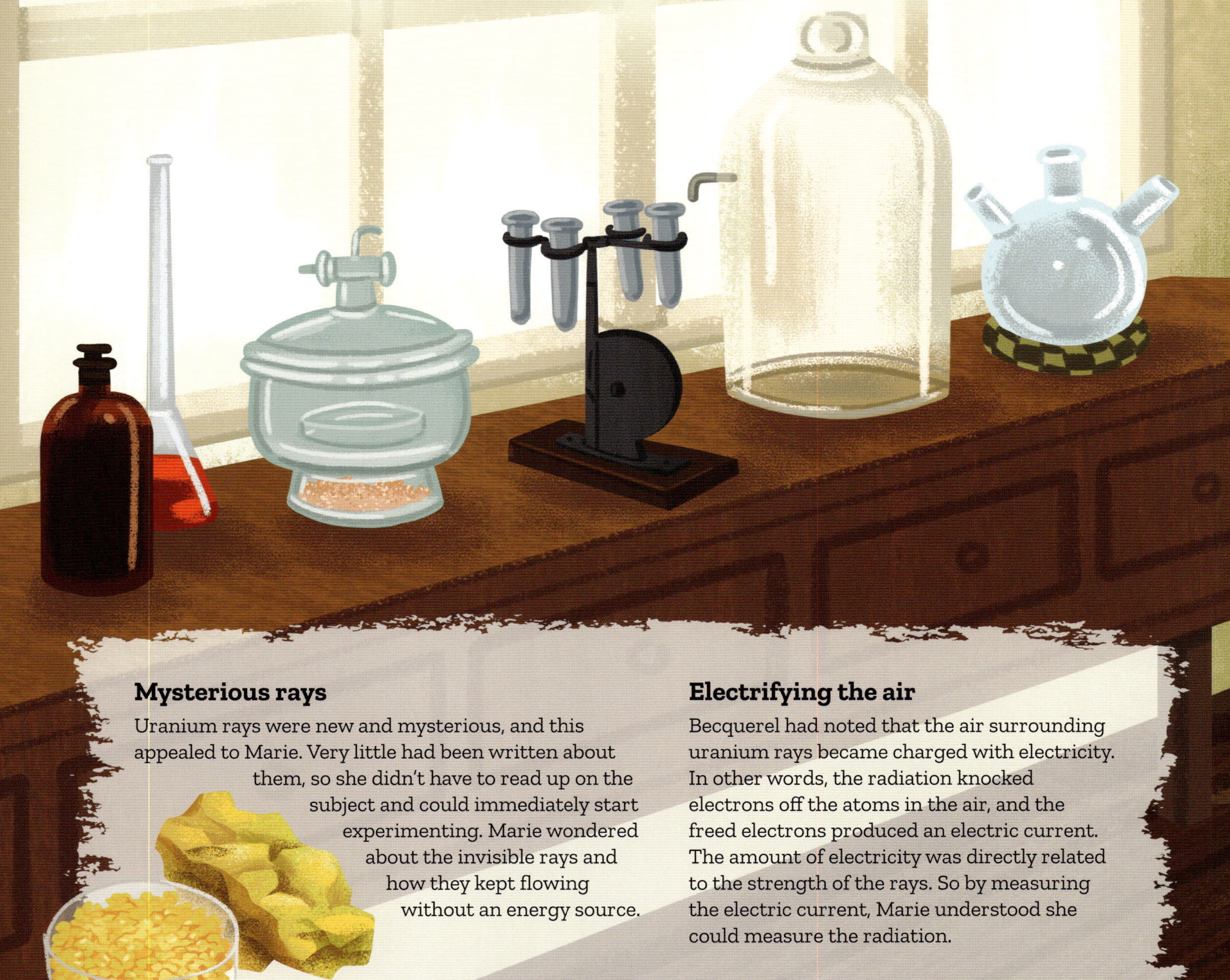

Mysterious rays

Uranium rays were new and mysterious, and this appealed to Marie. Very little had been written about them, so she didn't have to read up on the subject and could immediately start experimenting. Marie wondered about the invisible rays and how they kept flowing without an energy source.

Electrifying the air

Becquerel had noted that the air surrounding uranium rays became charged with electricity. In other words, the radiation knocked electrons off the atoms in the air, and the freed electrons produced an electric current. The amount of electricity was directly related to the strength of the rays. So by measuring the electric current, Marie understood she could measure the radiation.

Electrometer

By a happy coincidence, Pierre had the perfect device for her experiment. Fifteen years earlier, he and his older brother Jacques had invented an electrometer—a device that could measure electric currents in the air. The electrometer was highly sensitive and was able to make precise measurements of the tiny electrical changes that the uranium rays made as they passed through the air.

A new theory

Marie measured the rays from various uranium minerals. She discovered that the strength of the radiation did not depend on the mineral being studied, only on the amount of uranium it contained. From this, she concluded that the radiation could not be a result of the particular arrangement of molecules in the mineral—instead, it was coming from within the uranium atoms themselves.

A revolutionary idea

At the time, scientists believed that the atom was the fundamental or basic unit of matter and it could not be divided into anything smaller. The idea that something inside an atom could generate these rays was revolutionary. Marie had challenged the scientific understanding of the atom.

NOT JUST URANIUM

Marie Curie wanted to know if uranium was the only element that produced radiation or if others did, too. She experimented on many other minerals, testing all the known elements. In April 1898, she discovered an element called thorium that also emitted Becquerel rays.

BY COINCIDENCE, GERMAN CHEMIST GERHARD SCHMIDT DISCOVERED THAT THORIUM EMITTED BECQUEREL RAYS TWO MONTHS BEFORE MARIE CURIE.

Radioactivity

This proved that Becquerel's discovery was not unique to uranium. To describe the way uranium and thorium behaved, Marie coined the word radioactivity (see page 9). She wanted to see if other radioactive elements existed. Pierre helped with her research.

A new element?

One of the minerals that Marie tested was pitchblende, an ore (a rock containing useful metals or minerals) rich in uranium. The electrometer showed that pitchblende emitted four times as much radioactivity as could be explained by the uranium in it. She concluded that pitchblende must contain some other element, previously unheard of. She knew the amount of this element had to be tiny, since 99 percent of the substances in pitchblende had already been identified. Therefore, the new element must be much more radioactive than uranium.

MARIE WORKING WITH THE ELECTROMETER

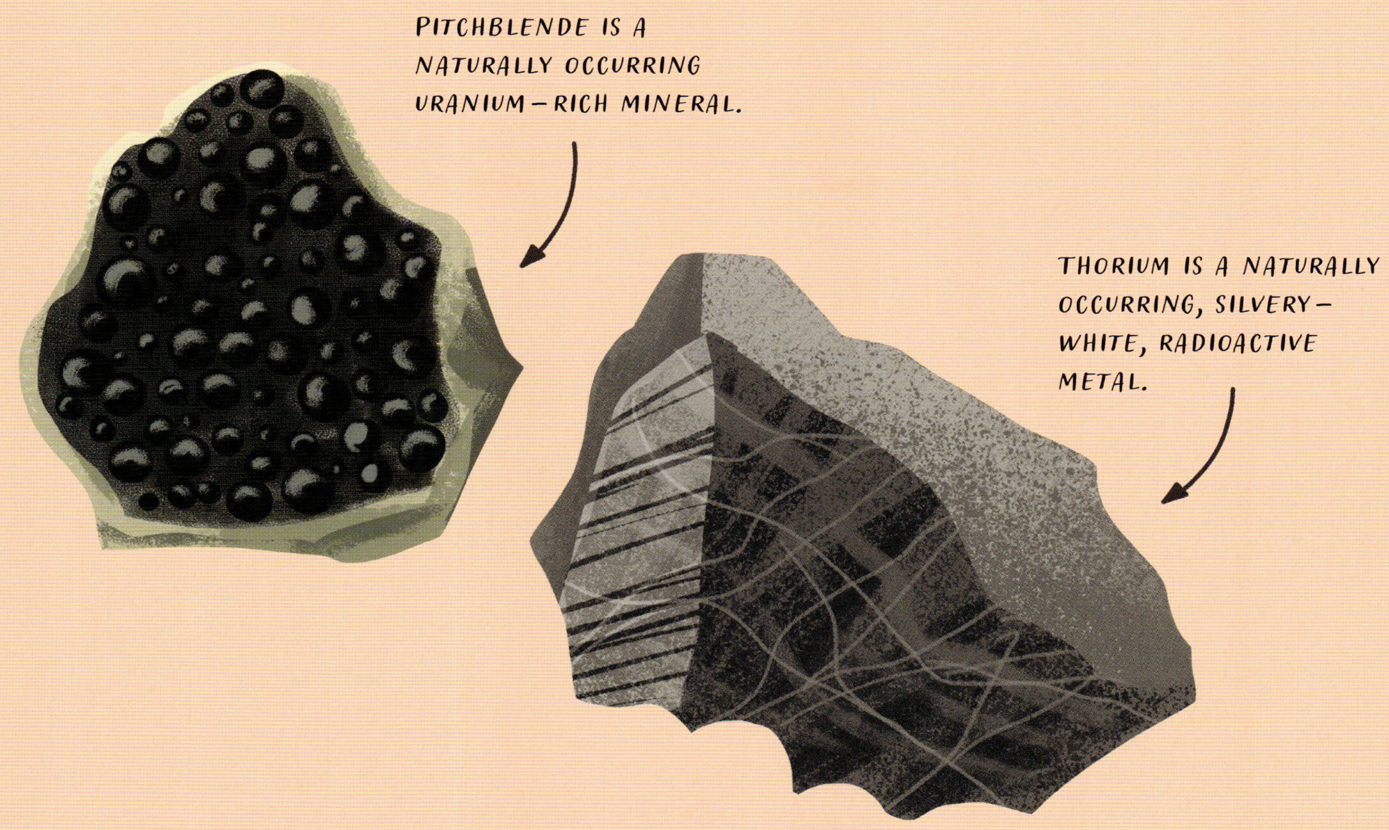

The testing process

Finding the new element was going to be tricky. Pitchblende contained around thirty elements. The Curies would have to separate all these different elements to find the one they were looking for. First they would grind up the pitchblende, then dissolve it in acid to separate it into its different fractions (clusters of similar elements). They would then test each fraction with the electrometer. The most radioactive ones would then be separated further. This process would be repeated again and again as they gradually homed in on the element they were looking for.

"There must be, I thought, some unknown substance, very active, in these minerals. My husband agreed with me and I urged that we search at once for this hypothetical substance, thinking that, with joined efforts, a result would be quickly obtained."
Marie Curie

THE DISCOVERY OF POLONIUM

The Curies found that one of the most radioactive fractions of pitchblende was rich in the element bismuth. Each time Marie removed some bismuth from the fraction, it became more radioactive. A new element had to be in there somewhere. By June 1898, the fraction was 300 times more radioactive than uranium. Finally, in July, the Curies managed to extract the elusive new element.

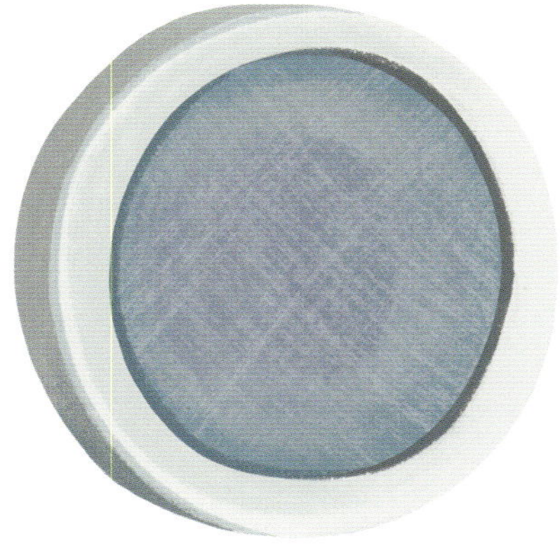

A THIN FILM OF POLONIUM ON A STAINLESS STEEL DISK

Remembering her homeland

This was the first element to be identified by its radioactivity, which was 400 times stronger than uranium. At first they called it "radium F," but then Marie decided to name it polonium after her native Poland. At the time, Poland was still under foreign occupation, and Marie hoped that naming the element after Poland might highlight the plight of her country.

Big announcement

Marie and Pierre announced their discovery in a paper published on July 18, 1898. They wrote: "We believe the substance we have extracted from pitchblende contains a metal not yet observed, akin to bismuth in its analytic properties. If the existence of this new metal is confirmed, we propose to call it polonium, from the name of the original country of one of us." In this paper, the word *radioactive* appeared in print for the first time.

MARIE AND PIERRE DISCOVERING POLONIUM

Another discovery

The residue left behind after the Curies had extracted the polonium was still highly radioactive, so they knew that yet another radioactive element existed in the pitchblende. This element was far more radioactive than polonium, but present in even smaller quantities. To find it they would need a much bigger quantity of pitchblende.

More pitchblende needed

At this time, the main source of pitchblende was a uranium mine in Bohemia in the Austro-Hungarian Empire. In September 1898, the Curies sent a request to the Austrian government, and in November, 100 kg (220 lb) of pitchblende was delivered to their laboratory. Marie and Pierre immediately went to work. This time, they focused on a different fraction of pitchblende, rich in the element barium. One month later, they found what they were looking for.

THE DISCOVERY OF RADIUM

On December 26, 1898, the Curies announced the discovery of a second new element. They named it radium from the Latin word for ray. It was 900 times more radioactive than polonium!

Persuading the scientific community

Many scientists did not believe that the Curies had found two brand-new elements in just five months. The Curies did not have enough polonium and radium to see and weigh, so the only evidence that these elements existed was their radioactivity. To prove to the scientific community that polonium and radium were real, the Curies would have to isolate them. In other words, they would have to separate them from the other substances they were mixed with to produce pure examples of each element.

Sample of pitchblende dissolved in nitric acid in a flask, to separate out the different ingredients. Pitchblende and nitric acid combine to form uranyl nitrate, which is fluorescent, meaning it glows with light.

Help from Austria

From their experiments, the Curies worked out that the proportion of polonium and radium in pitchblende was less than a millionth of one percent! They would therefore need a truly enormous quantity of pitchblende if they were to isolate even a tiny amount of the new elements. Fortunately, the President of the Academy of Sciences in Austria understood the importance of the Curies' work. He was able to convince the Austrian government to supply the Curies with several tons of pitchblende at a reasonable price.

Lab in a shed

The Curies' laboratory wasn't big enough to store and process such a large quantity of the mineral, so they were given the use of a shed behind the Sorbonne's School of Physics and Chemistry. Marie ground the pitchblende to powder, then put it in huge pots together with chemicals to help break it down. She stirred and cooked the boiling mass with a heavy iron rod nearly as tall as she was.

The problem with polonium

Marie never succeeded in isolating pure polonium. This is because polonium decays rapidly due to its radioactivity. It has a half-life of just 138 days (the time it takes for half of the radioactive atoms in a substance to decay). So even as she was performing her separations, the polonium in her raw material was decaying. Instead, she focused her efforts on isolating radium.

ISOLATING RADIUM

Radium existed in the barium fraction (the part of pitchblende rich in barium). It took the Curies four long years to separate a small amount of radium from the barium fraction. Even this wasn't pure radium, but radium salts (radium chloride). However, it was enough to prove that radium existed as an element.

A long process

The first stage was to extract substances known as alkalines from the barium fraction by dissolving it in acid. The Curies then used a process called crystallization to extract radium chloride from the alkalines. Thousands of crystallizations were necessary to complete the process.

Hazardous conditions

The shed where the Curies worked was old and dilapidated. It had broken windows and a glass roof that leaked when it rained. The shed was filled with giant cauldrons where they dissolved the barium fraction. There were no chimneys to take away the poisonous gases produced by their activities. On dry days they would work in the courtyard next to the shed for some fresh air. It was an exhausting process, moving containers, pouring liquids, and stirring for hours at a time.

Pure radium

In September 1910, Marie Curie and French chemist André-Louis Debierne succeeded in isolating radium as a pure metal. First they used a process called electrolysis to convert radium chloride into an alloy (mixture) of radium and mercury. They then heated the alloy to remove the mercury, leaving pure radium.

"One of our pleasures was to enter our workshop at night. Then, all around us, we would see the luminous silhouettes of the beakers and capsules that contained our products."

Marie Curie

THE LITTLE CURIES

When World War I broke out, Marie Curie was determined to find a way of using her scientific knowledge to help soldiers in battle. Her radiology cars, popularly known in French as ***petites Curies*** ("little Curies"), made a significant contribution to battlefield care.

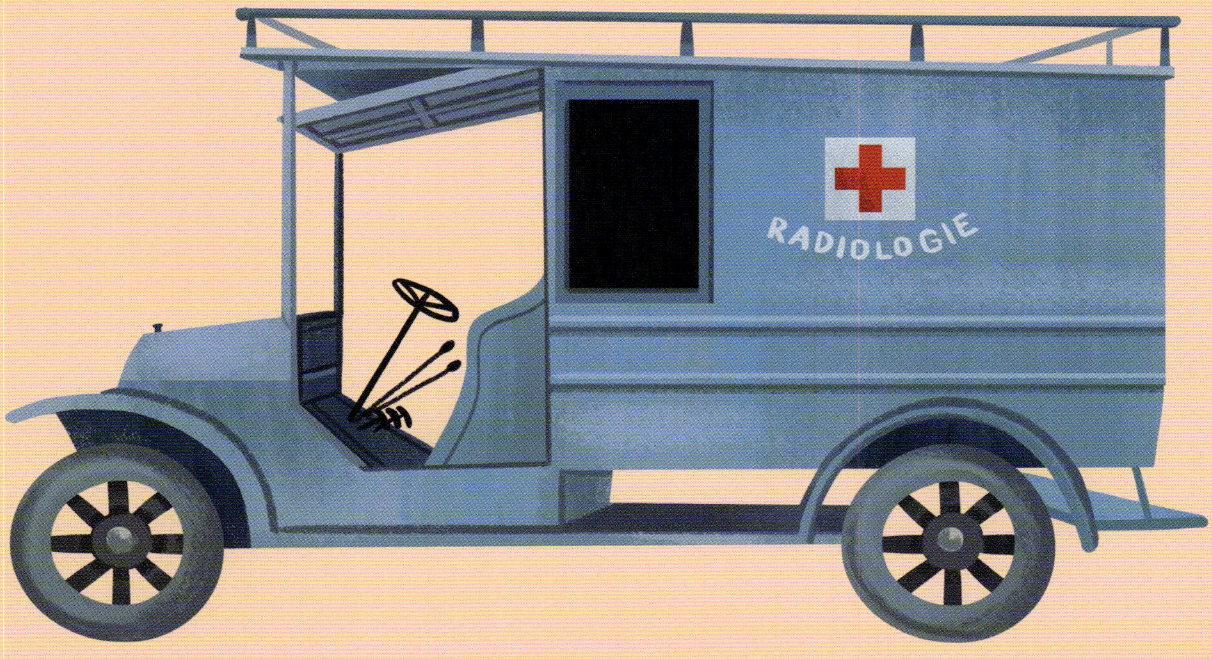

The need for speed

In war, speed is critical for treating wounded soldiers, and military surgeons were often forced to operate with limited knowledge of internal injuries. Marie's mobile radiology units brought cutting-edge X-ray technology to the front line, helping surgeons quickly identify injury locations within a patient's body.

Challenges

Marie faced formidable challenges in bringing her plan to fruition. Her understanding of radiology was limited, she was not a doctor, and she knew nothing about cars. At the start of the war, X-ray technology was still quite new. The machines that existed were only available in large city hospitals, and most of them were big and not easily portable. It took someone with Marie's imagination, determination, and organization skills to create a fleet of mobile X-ray units. She was helped by many talented and dedicated people, including medical experts, engineers, and volunteers from the Red Cross and the Union of French Women.

Portable machine

To equip her first vehicle, Marie acquired a portable X-ray machine, which was the invention of a Spanish engineer named Mónico Sánchez Moreno. Moreno's machine produced X-rays using a cathode-ray tube, which required a source of electricity. Marie provided this by attaching a dynamo (an electricity generator) to the vehicle's engine.

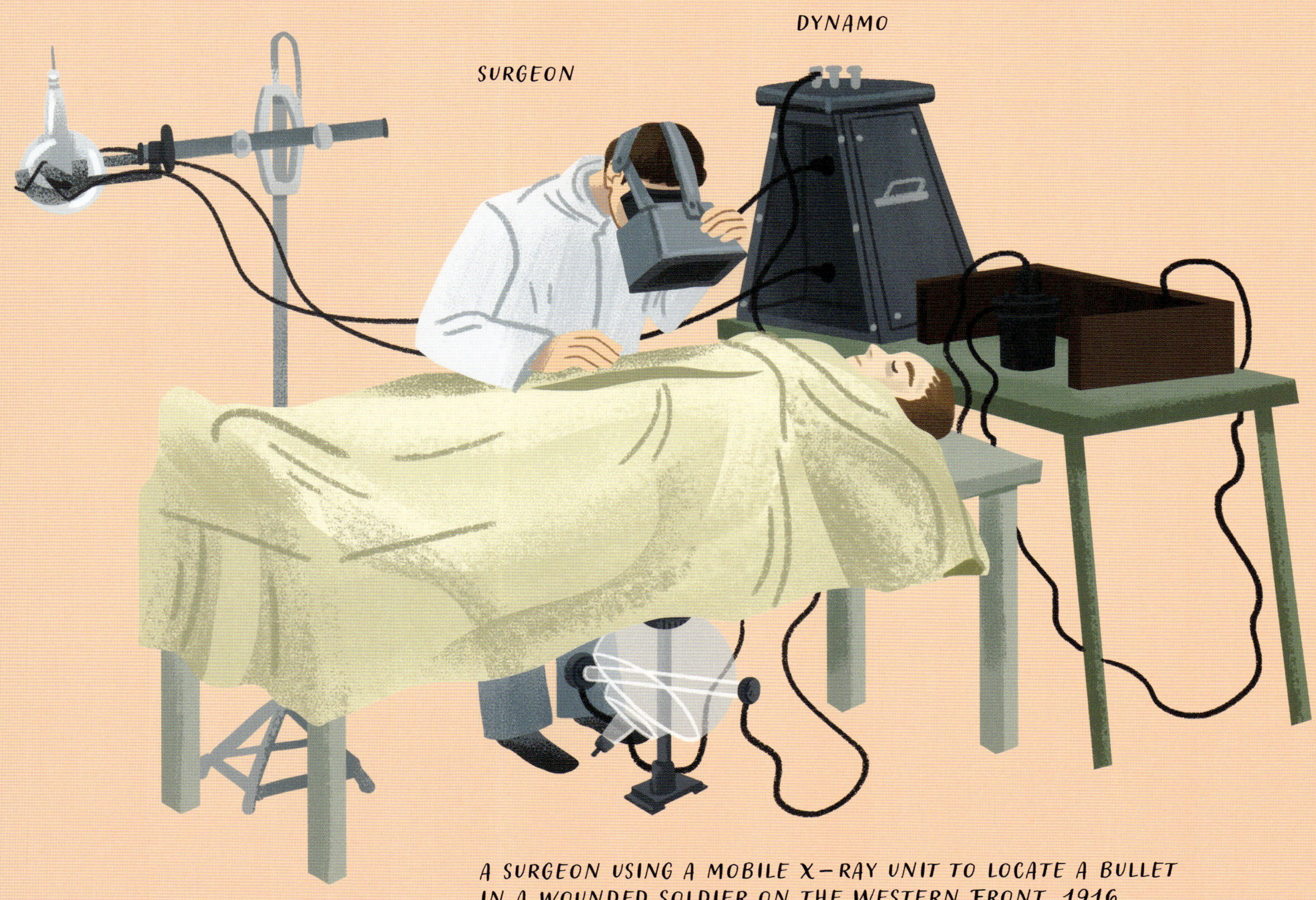

A SURGEON USING A MOBILE X-RAY UNIT TO LOCATE A BULLET IN A WOUNDED SOLDIER ON THE WESTERN FRONT, 1916

The fleet

Over time, and with the financial support of friends, Marie went on to equip twenty little Curies, each of which contained a little darkroom where X-ray photographs could be developed. The vehicles also featured a portable fluoroscope—an instrument for viewing X-rays without needing to develop them as photographs.

"The dominant duty imposed on everyone at that time was to help the country in whatever way possible during the extreme crisis that it faced."
Marie Curie

CURIE'S LEGACY

UNDERSTANDING THE ATOM

With her discovery that radiation comes from inside atoms, Marie Curie helped disprove the old idea that atoms are indivisible. She proved that atoms had an internal structure and that particles within it were emitted as radiation. The remaining questions were—what was that internal structure, and how did these particles fit into it?

Discovering the electron

In April 1897, a few months before Marie Curie began her study of uranium rays, English physicist J. J. Thomson discovered the electron—a particle 1,000 times lighter than the atom. This discovery proved that particles even smaller than atoms existed.

Plum pudding model

Thomson's experiments suggested that electrons exist within atoms. Electrons are negatively charged particles, yet atoms have a neutral charge. To explain how this was possible, in 1904, Thomson came up with his "plum pudding" model of the atom. He imagined the atom as a positive field with negative electrons stuck within it like plums in a pudding. The positive and negative charges cancel each other out, giving the atom its neutral charge.

"The atom is not unchanging and indivisible, since its particles are radiated out."
Marie Curie

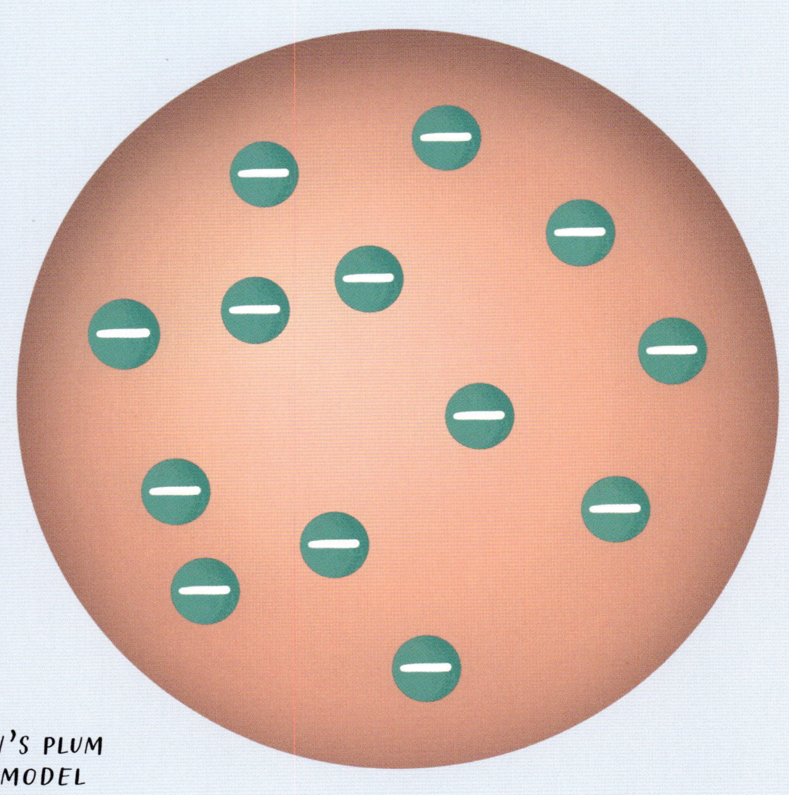

THOMSON'S PLUM PUDDING MODEL

Rutherford's experiment

In 1905, New Zealand physicist Ernest Rutherford tested Thomson's plum pudding model. Building on Marie Curie's research, Rutherford discovered that radioactive atoms emit different kinds of radiation. One of these, which he called alpha particles, had a positive charge. Rutherford fired a beam of alpha particles at a very thin piece of gold foil.

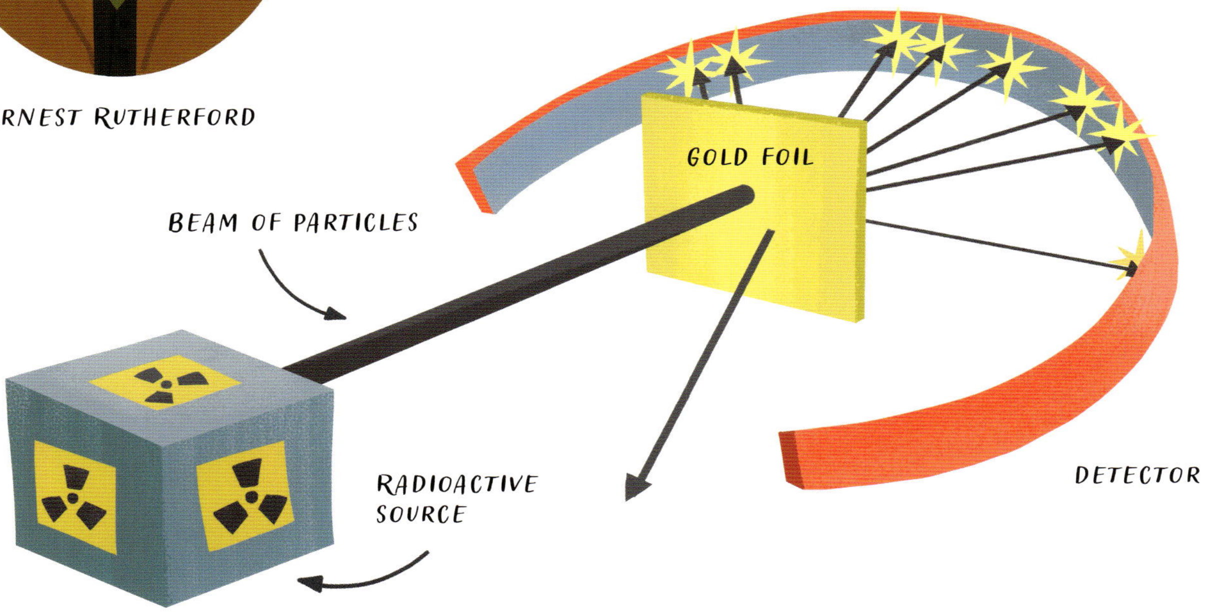

ERNEST RUTHERFORD

GOLD FOIL

BEAM OF PARTICLES

RADIOACTIVE SOURCE

DETECTOR

A surprising result

Most of the alpha particles flew straight through the foil, suggesting that atoms are mainly empty space. A very small number were deflected at a large angle or flew straight back. Since positive charges repel each other, these alpha particles must have hit something positively charged. As there were so few that did this, however, the positive charge in the atom must be concentrated in a tiny core (nucleus). Rutherford proposed a new model of the atom, with a tiny, dense, positively charged nucleus surrounded by electrons. Rutherford's model wasn't complete, but it was another key step toward understanding the atom.

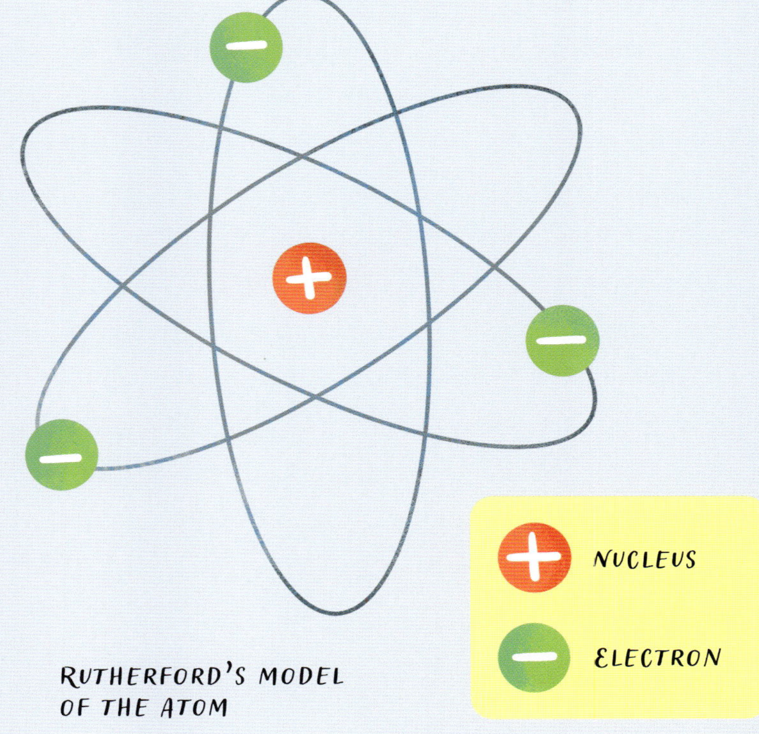

RUTHERFORD'S MODEL OF THE ATOM

THE CURIE METHOD

The Curies developed a uniquely accurate method for measuring the radioactivity of substances, helping them discover the new elements polonium and radium. The method involved three main pieces of equipment—an ionization chamber, a quadrant electrometer, and a piezoelectric quartz electrometer.

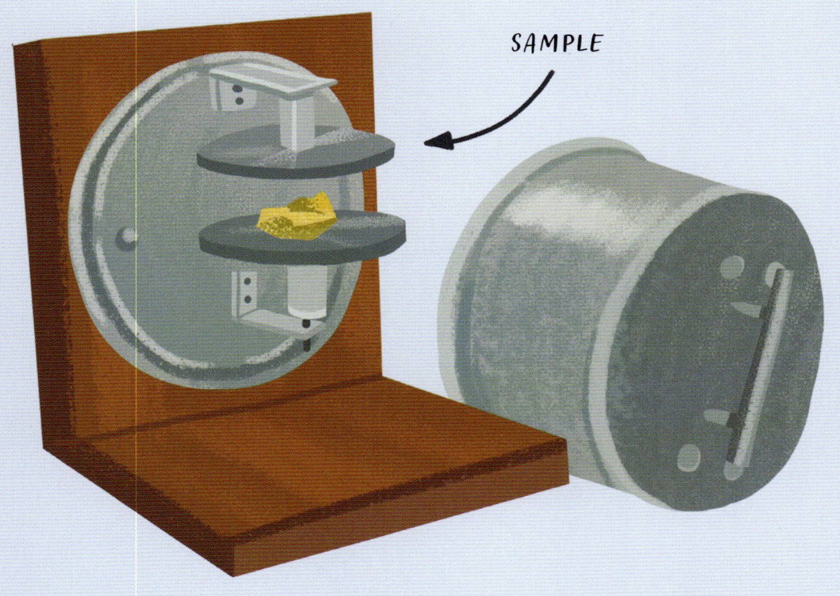

Ionization chamber

To test its radioactivity, the Curies would place the sample in an ionization chamber, which consisted of two electrically charged plates connected to a power source. If the sample was radioactive, it would electrically charge the air between the plates. Negative electrons would flow to the positive plate, creating an electric current within the chamber.

Quadrant electrometer

To measure the electric charge created by the sample in the ionization chamber, the Curies used a quadrant electrometer. Inside this device is a small, round mirror rotated by an electric charge. The Curies projected a beam of light onto the mirror, which was reflected onto a ruler. As the mirror rotated, the light slowly moved along the ruler. Marie used a stopwatch to measure the time it took for the light to move from one point to another. The faster it moved, the more radioactive the sample was. By itself, the quadrant electrometer could not produce accurate measurements. Marie needed another instrument.

Piezoelectric quartz electrometer

In 1880, Pierre and his brother Jacques Curie discovered that when quartz is compressed, it generates an electric charge. They called this piezoelectricity. The greater the pressure on the quartz, the more electricity it generates. They invented the piezoelectric quartz electrometer to measure this electric charge. Marie saw she could use this device to provide a benchmark for her radioactivity measurements. She could compare the known charge of the quartz to the charge produced by the radioactive sample. This was Marie's great innovation.

An eagle eye

Marie followed a little spot of light moving across a ruler with only her eyes. Her careful technique, despite difficult laboratory conditions, ensured the accuracy of her measurements. The Curie Method continued to be used for over fifty years to measure the radioactivity of minerals. It was eventually replaced by the Geiger counter; however, it is still used in educational demonstrations.

CANCER TREATMENT

Soon after they discovered radium, Marie and Pierre realized it could be used to treat cancer. They saw that the radiation emitted by radium destroyed diseased cells faster than healthy cells. Their work led to the development of radiotherapy, which remains one of the main treatments for cancer to this day.

Radiotherapy

Radiotherapy (RT) can shrink tumors (cancerous lumps in the body) or at least slow down their growth, improving the quality of life for cancer patients. Two thirds of cancer patients will receive RT at some point during their care. It is often combined with chemotherapy (medicines) and surgery. The Radium Institute, founded by Marie Curie, pioneered radiotherapy techniques.

External beam radiation

The most common form of RT is external beam radiation. Rays emitted by a machine are focused on the part of the patient's body where the tumor is located. They pass through the skin to reach the tumor.

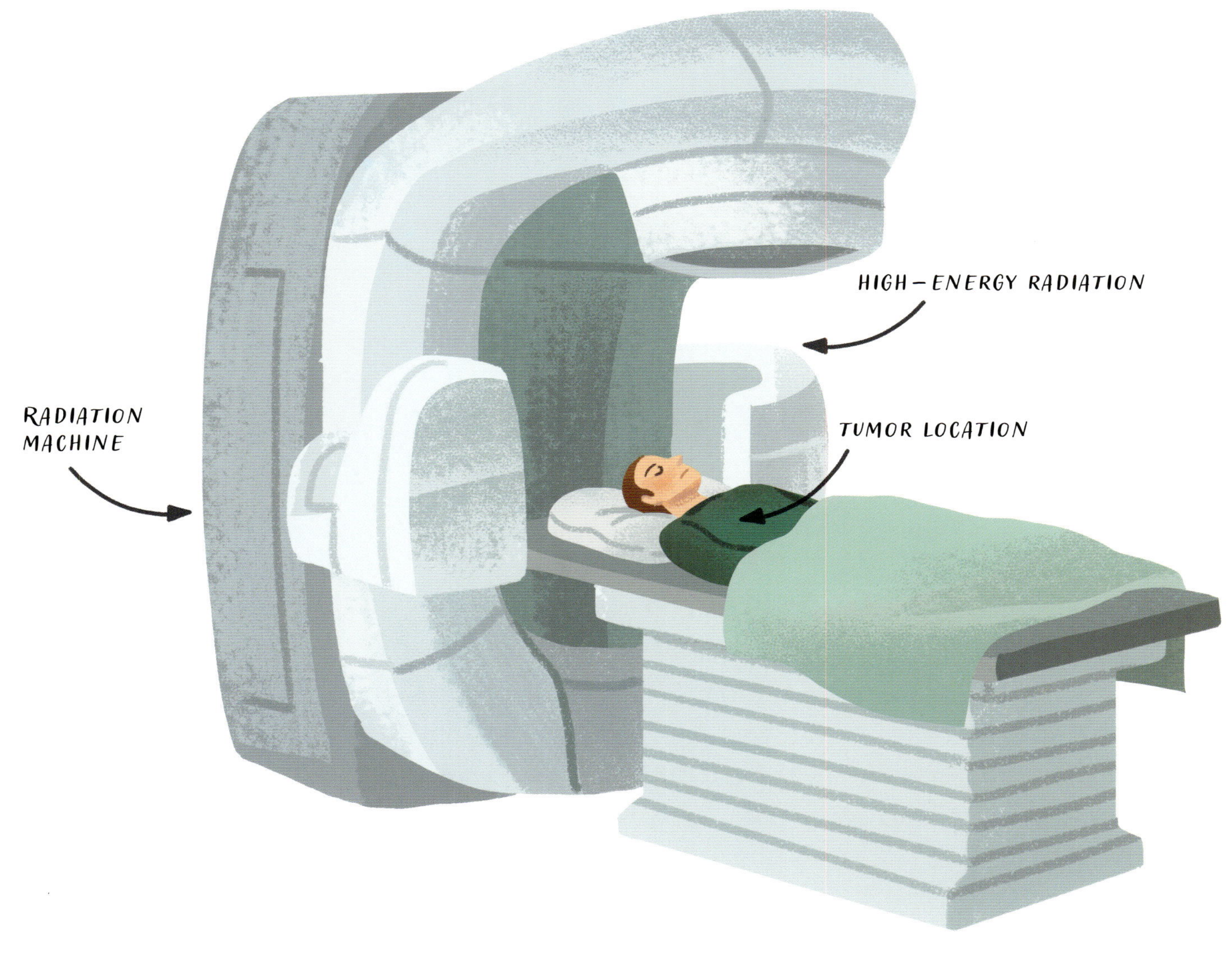

Curietherapy

Brachytherapy (BT), also known as curietherapy, is an RT technique in which a tiny piece of radioactive material, known as a seed, is inserted inside or beside a tumor. This allows high doses of radiation to be delivered directly to the tumor, minimizing damage to surrounding tissue. This is particularly useful for treating breast, cervical, prostate, lung, and brain cancer. The Curies provided the radium for the very first BT treatment in 1901.

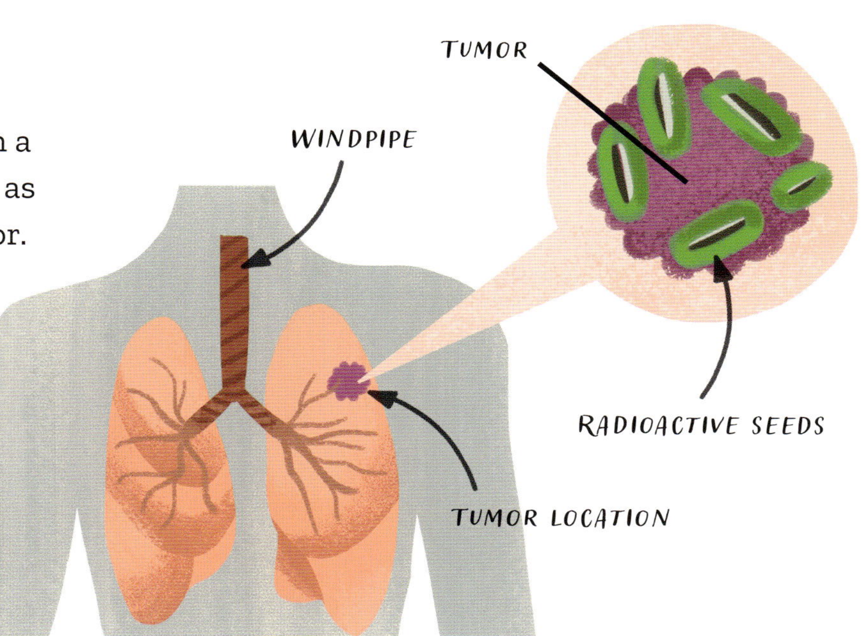

Marie Curie Hospital

During the 1920s, a group of British medical women, inspired by the work of Marie Curie, opened a hospital. They launched a public campaign and raised the funds to purchase a large building in London. Marie Curie was interested in the project and agreed to give her name to the hospital. The Marie Curie Hospital for Cancer and Allied Diseases opened in 1929.

MARIE CURIE HOSPITAL IN HAMPSTEAD, LONDON, AS IT LOOKED IN THE 1930S

The thirty-bed hospital was staffed entirely by women and offered the latest RT treatments, including external beam radiation and brachytherapy. By the 1960s, the hospital lacked the facilities to keep up with modern developments in cancer treatment and was moved to a ward in a nearby hospital. The Marie Curie Hospital closed in 1967.

NUCLEAR MEDICINE

Marie Curie's research into radioactivity led indirectly to the development of a new technique to diagnose diseases. Nuclear medicine involves injecting the patient with a radioactive substance called a radiotracer. The radiotracer emits a signal that is measured by highly sensitive equipment, which can convert it into an image.

The Curies' contribution

Nuclear medicine is based on the principle that Marie Curie first explored—that the radioactivity of substances can be measured and recorded. The discoveries of her daughter and son-in-law, Irène and Frédéric Joliot-Curie, in the 1930s led to the development of radiotracers in the 1940s and the beginning of nuclear medicine.

Understanding organ function

Radiotracers have no side effects and the amount of radiation absorbed by the body during a nuclear medicine scan is generally lower than that of an X-ray. Unlike most types of scans, such as X-rays, which show how the inside of the body looks, nuclear medicine scans show how organs function. This helps doctors make a diagnosis and plan treatments.

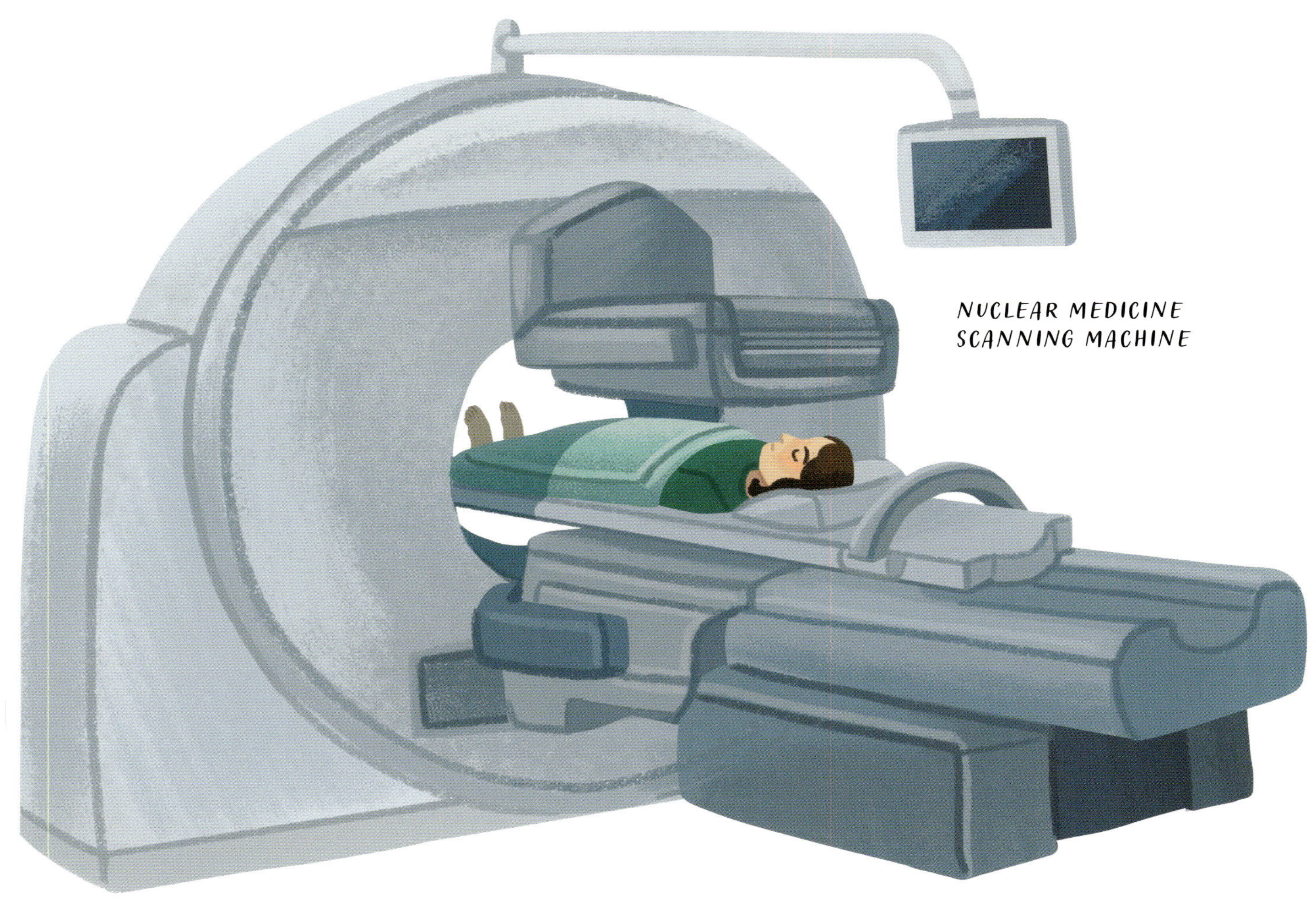

SPECT scanner

One common form of nuclear medicine is Single Photon Emission Computed Tomography (SPECT). The SPECT scanner has camera sensors that can detect gamma ray emissions from radiotracers in different parts of the body. The cameras are mounted on a rotating structure that moves in a circle around the patient, recording their body from different angles. A computer then converts this data into a 3D image. SPECT scans are mainly used to diagnose and track the progress of heart, bone, and gallbladder diseases.

PET scanner

Positron Emission Tomography (PET) is another kind of nuclear medicine technique. Whereas SPECT scans measure gamma rays, PET scans measure tiny particles called positrons. A positron has roughly the same mass as an electron, but it has a positive charge. When positrons react with electrons in the body, they destroy each other. This destruction produces energy in the form of two photons (light particles) that shoot off in opposite directions. Detectors in the PET scanner measure these photons and use this to create images of internal organs. PET scans are mainly used to detect cancer and monitor its progress.

PET SCANS ARE ALSO USED TO DIAGNOSE ALZHEIMER'S DISEASE.

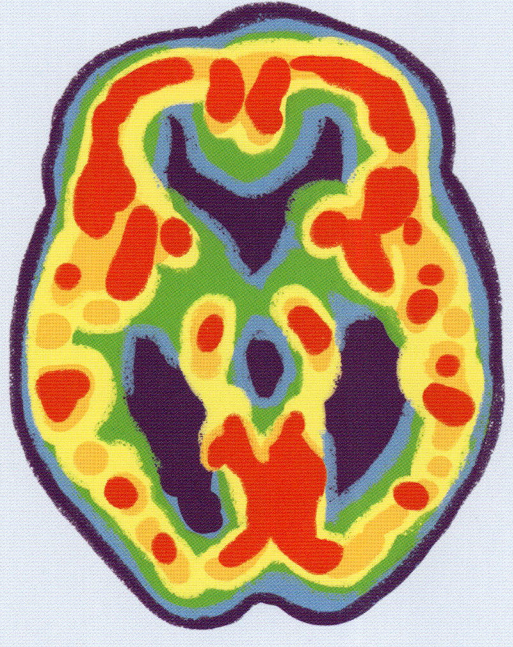

SCAN OF A HEALTHY HUMAN BRAIN

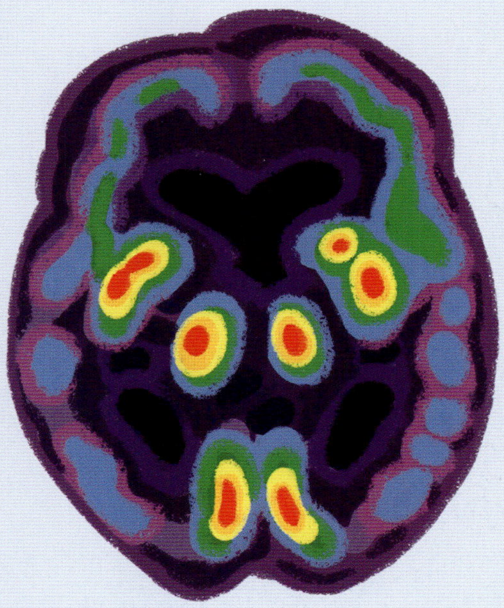

SCAN OF A BRAIN WITH ALZHEIMER'S DISEASE

NUCLEAR ENERGY

Marie Curie's research on radioactivity, especially her insight that radiation comes from processes within the atom, opened the door to the development of nuclear energy. In the 1930s and 1940s, scientists began researching nuclear energy, which is energy that could be released by splitting the atoms of radioactive elements, such as uranium. This was seen as a potential source of electric power and also as a possible weapon.

Nuclear fission

The process of splitting the nucleus of an atom to release energy is called nuclear fission. A number of scientists worked on nuclear fission, including Marie Curie's son-in-law, Frédéric Joliot-Curie. They discovered that firing a neutron at an atom of uranium-235 (an isotope of uranium) will split the atom's nucleus into two lighter elements.

Chain reaction

The process of splitting the nucleus also releases two or three neutrons. These neutrons will hit other nearby uranium-235 atoms, which will also split, generating more neutrons. Thus, the splitting of one nucleus sets off others in a chain reaction. All this occurs in a fraction of a second.

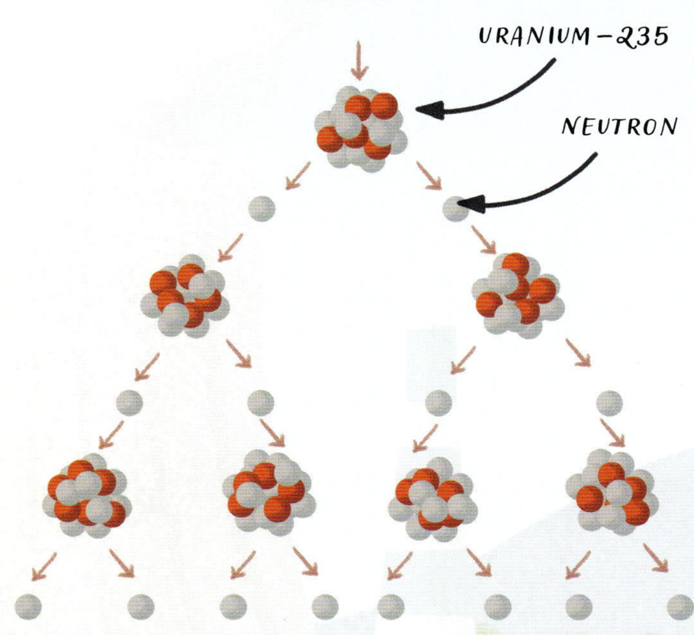

Electric power

In a nuclear power station, nuclear fission chain reactions are carefully controlled to produce a steady amount of electric power. In the nuclear reactor, rods of a radioactive element (usually uranium-238) are bundled together. They are immersed in water to slow down and control the reaction. The heat created by nuclear fission turns the water to steam, which spins a turbine to produce electricity. In 1947, Frédéric Joliot-Curie began designing France's first nuclear reactor. The Zoé Reactor, as it was known, began operating on December 15, 1948.

Atomic bomb

Scientists developed nuclear fission shortly before the start of World War II (1939–1945), and governments quickly saw that this process could be used to make a bomb. The atomic bomb works on the same principle as nuclear power stations, except that the chain reaction is extremely rapid and uncontrolled, causing a massive explosion. In first atomic bomb, only 1 kg (2 lb) of the 64 kg (141 lb) of uranium-235 used became energy. But this energy was the equivalent to around 16,000-plus tons of TNT—a powerful explosive chemical compound.

RADIOMETRIC DATING

Marie Curie was the first person to suggest that radioactivity was linked to activity occurring inside the atom. In 1900, New Zealand physicist Ernest Rutherford, working with radioactive materials supplied to him by Curie, looked in more detail at this process. He concluded that the isotopes of radioactive elements are unstable and decay over time into stable isotopes of the same element or different elements. As they do so, they emit radiation.

Half-life

In 1904, Rutherford invented the term "half-life." This refers to the amount of time it takes for half of the atoms in a sample of a radioactive isotope to decay into a stable isotope. Rutherford noticed that every radioactive isotope has a particular half-life. For example, the isotope radium-226 has a half-life of 1,600 years—that's the time it takes for half the atoms in a radium-226 sample to decay into the stable isotope radon-222. In 1906, Marie Curie confirmed Rutherford's decay theory.

Radioactive decay

UNSTABLE ISOTOPE

STABLE ISOTOPE

0 HALF-LIVES: NO ATOMS HAVE DECAYED

1 HALF-LIFE: HALF THE ATOMS HAVE DECAYED

2 HALF-LIVES: THREE QUARTERS OF THE ATOMS HAVE DECAYED

Dating rocks and fossils

Rutherford's discovery was useful because it meant that radioactive isotopes are like natural clocks in the earth. Scientists can work out the age of any rock or fossil containing a radioactive isotope based on how many of its atoms have decayed. This technique is known as radiometric dating. Using this method, scientists even managed to work out the age of the Earth (4.6 billion years old) by analyzing uranium-238, which has a very long half-life of 4.5 billion years—the time it takes for half its atoms to decay into lead.

JURASSIC AMMONITE FOSSIL (170 MILLION YEARS OLD)

Radiocarbon dating

Living organisms absorb the isotope carbon-14 (radioactive carbon) from the air and food. Once an organism dies, it stops absorbing carbon-14. The carbon-14 in the organism's tissues starts to decay into the stable isotope of carbon-12 at a steady rate over time. (It has a half-life of 5,730 years.) By measuring the amount of carbon-14 in a sample, scientists can calculate the sample's age. This is called radiocarbon dating. It's a valuable tool to date animal and plant remains up to 60,000 years old.

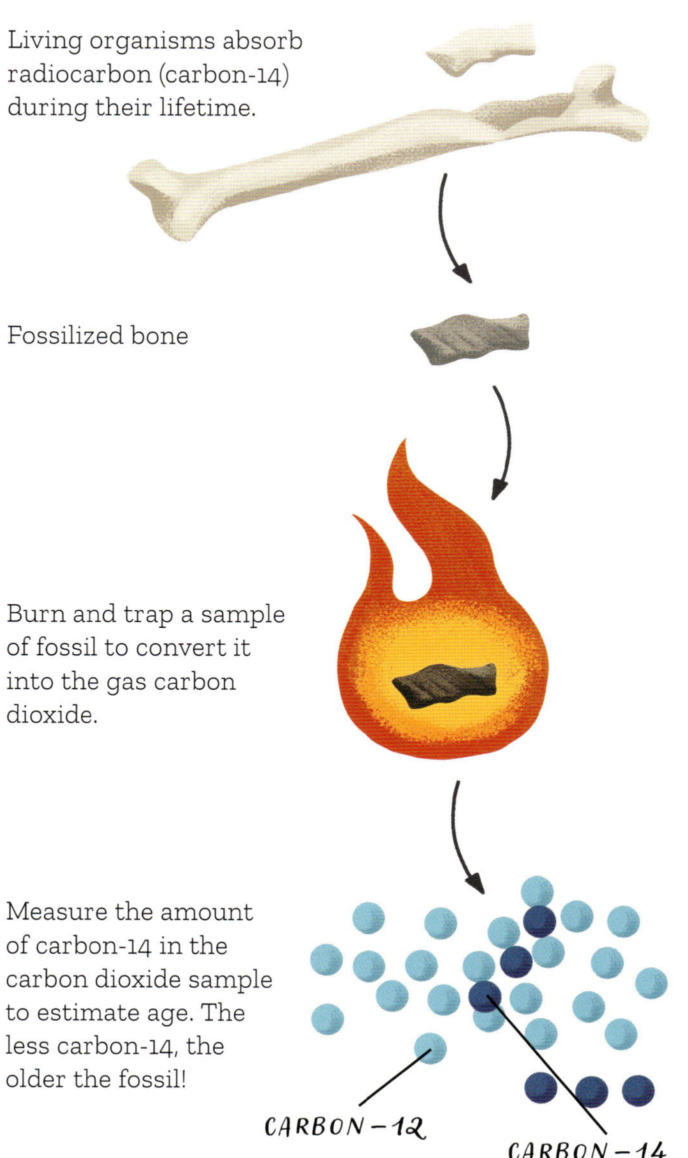

USES OF POLONIUM

Polonium, discovered by the Curies in 1898, is a rare element with no stable isotopes. It occurs naturally as the highly radioactive isotope polonium-210, which has a half-life of just 138 days. Polonium-210 emits alpha particles, which carry high amounts of energy that can damage or destroy the cells in our bodies. In its pure form, polonium is a silvery metalloid (a substance with both metallic and nonmetallic properties).

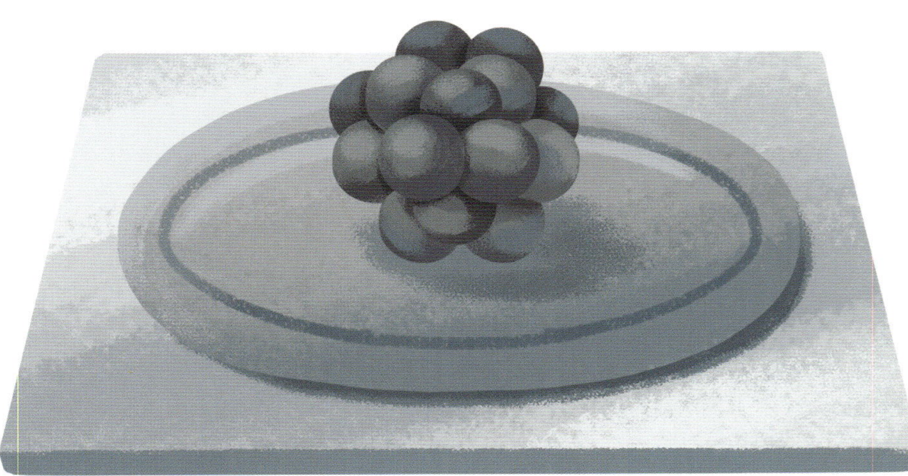

POLONIUM-210

Antistatic

Static electricity is a buildup of electric charge in an object. For example, when you comb your hair, the friction can cause electrons to move from your hair to the comb, leaving your hair with a positive charge and the comb with a negative charge. Polonium-210 emits alpha particles, which strips electrons from the atoms in the air, creating ions (atoms with a positive or negative charge). The ions neutralize the static electric charge. Polonium is therefore a useful component for antistatic brushes to remove static from materials, such as photographic film.

Space power

Despite being rare, difficult to produce, and highly dangerous to humans, polonium has a number of uses. Because of its short half-life, its decay generates a lot of heat. One gram of Polonium-210 will spontaneously heat to above 500 °C (932 °F), generating about 140 watts of power. This made it useful as a heat source in space exploration. In the 1970s, the Soviet Union used polonium to keep their lunar rovers warm. However, since then space missions have used plutonium-238, which provides more sustained power.

Neutron sources

A neutron source is a device that generates neutrons. Polonium is often used in neutron sources because it emits alpha particles that, when combined with another element, such as beryllium, will produce neutrons. Neutron sources are used in many different fields, including industry, medicine, scientific research, and nuclear power.

Nuclear weapons

Polonium was used as part of the trigger mechanism for the first atomic bomb which was dropped on the Japanese city of Nagasaki in 1945 in World War II. Polonium was combined with beryllium to generate neutrons, which then started a nuclear fission chain reaction.

USES OF RADIUM

After the Curies discovered radium in 1898, this mysterious glowing element sparked something of a craze with the public. Soon, radium was appearing as a luminous paint for watches, clocks, and instrument dials, and as an additive in toothpaste, hair creams, and even foods. Doctors used radium as a treatment for cancer, acne, varicose veins, epilepsy, and many other conditions. These products and treatments soon became unpopular when the health risks of radium were discovered.

RADIUM GLOWING IN A FLASK NEXT TO A CHUNK OF PITCHBLENDE

Dangers

Radium is a highly radioactive metal. Exposure to radium, whether by ingesting it or rubbing it on the skin, can cause cancer and other disorders. Radium emits alpha particles and gamma rays as it decays, which destroy and mutate (change) cells. As a result, radium consumer products had disappeared by the 1960s. Today, it is used mainly in scientific research, industry, and some cancer treatments.

COSMETICS AND SOME PERSONAL CARE ITEMS, SUCH AS TOOTHPASTE, ONCE CONTAINED RADIUM.

Industrial radiography

Radium is sometimes used as a source of gamma rays in order to test materials for any hidden flaws. These might be pipelines, building materials, storage tanks, boilers, or vehicle and aircraft parts. The technique, known as industrial radiography, works as follows: a beam of radiation is directed at the material being tested. On the other side of the material, a detector records the radiation passing through the material. The detector then creates an image from this data that shows any cracks or flaws.

Clocks

Radium is finding a new use in a cutting-edge clock called a trapped ion optical clock. This highly accurate clock works by capturing and trapping a single radium ion (charged atom) in a vacuum. It then uses laser beams to extract time and frequency information from the trapped ions. The unique qualities of the radium-226 isotope make it an ideal choice for this device.

Cancer treatment

The isotope radium-223 is sometimes used to treat prostate cancer that has spread to the bones. Bones contain calcium, and radium has similar properties to calcium—it builds up in bone and especially in bone tumors. For this reason, radium-223 can be used to target cancerous bone cells. Radium-223 gives off alpha particles that can kill the cancerous cells.

THE RADIUM INSTITUTE

The Radium Institute, later known as the Curie Institute, is one of Marie Curie's most enduring legacies. The original Radium Institute consisted of the Curie Laboratory, directed by Marie Curie and which focused on physics and chemistry research into radioactivity; and the Pasteur Laboratory, led by Dr. Claudius Regaud, which studied the biological and medical effects of radioactivity.

Radiology

During World War I, Curie used the Radium Institute to teach nurses and technicians about radiology. During the 1920s, a healthcare clinic established at the Institute developed new treatments combining surgery and radiation therapy to treat cancer.

Research

Curie organized the Radium Institute into small teams of researchers, each tackling different questions about radioactivity. Right up until her death, she kept tabs on the work of each team, taking time to talk to the researchers whenever she came in. Under her leadership, the Radium Institute became an international hub for the study of radioactivity. It was here that, in 1934, Irène Curie and her husband Frédéric Joliot discovered artificial radioactivity, for which they won the Nobel Prize in Chemistry the following year. Between 1919 and Curie's death in 1934, scientists at the Institute published 483 works, including 31 books and papers by Curie herself.

Stockpiling radioactive elements

Marie Curie understood the need to stockpile radioactive elements for scientific research. The Radium Institute possessed a stock of 1.5 grams of radium. This was used in experiments in the late 1920s and early 1930s, including those performed by Irène Curie and Frédéric Joliot. English physicist James Chadwick built on this work which led to the discovery of the neutron in 1932, another key step in our understanding of the atom.

Curie Institute

In 1970, the Radium Institute combined with the Curie Foundation to become the new Curie Institute. Today, its research focuses on biophysics, cell biology, and oncology (cancer treatment), and it includes a hospital specializing in the treatment of cancer. Among its researchers are six Nobel Prize winners and many pioneering female scientists. Marie Curie herself mentored some forty-five female scientists, including Marguerite Perey, discoverer of francium, and Jeanne Ferrier, discoverer of autoradiography.

A PIONEER FOR WOMEN IN SCIENCE

Marie Curie was not only a great scientist but also a trailblazer for women in science. When Marie was a little girl, it was unusual for women to get the opportunity to make great scientific discoveries. It is a tribute to her intelligence, ambition, and determination that she achieved what she did—overcoming social barriers to become one of the most renowned scientists in history.

Blazing a trail

When Marie Curie became the first woman to win a Nobel Prize in 1903, it represented a major breakthrough not just for her but for women in general. It's no surprise she became an icon for generations of female scientists that followed, including her daughter Irène Joliot-Curie (see pages 28–29), who went on to win a Nobel Prize for Chemistry.

Inspiring others

With her discoveries, Curie lit the path for many female scientists. English chemist Dorothy Hodgkin was inspired by Curie's research on radiation and made her own discoveries in biology. She worked out the structure of molecules, such as penicillin and insulin. Another English chemist, Rosalind Franklin, contributed to the understanding of the structure of the DNA molecule, using principles established by Curie. Italian scientist Rita Levi-Montalcini won a Nobel Prize for her discoveries about nerve cells. Her work was aided by radiobiology, a field that emerged from Curie's research.

Promoting women

Marie Curie didn't just inspire women—she actively promoted them whenever she could. When she set up her radiology service during World War I, she made sure that women were trained as radiologists alongside men. At her Radium Institute in Paris, women made up 25–30 percent of researchers. By contrast, there were very few or no women at other scientific institutions at the time.

Enduring legacy

Today, record numbers of girls are studying STEM subjects, and women are well represented in scientific institutions around the world. This is at least in part thanks to a young Polish woman who was determined to let nothing stop her from pursuing her dream of becoming a scientist.

GLOSSARY

ALLOY—A metal made by combining two or more elements, usually to make it stronger or give it useful properties.

ALPHA PARTICLE—A particle made of two protons and two neutrons. It is given off during radioactive decay and has a positive charge.

ANATOMY—The study of the structure of living things, especially the parts of the human body.

ATOM—The smallest part of a chemical element.

ATOMIC BOMB—A bomb that gets its destructive power from the rapid release of nuclear energy by the fission (splitting) of atomic nuclei.

AUTORADIOGRAPHY—A technique that uses photographic film to detect radioactive substances in a sample.

BETA PARTICLE—A high-speed electron that is emitted from the nucleus of an atom during radioactive decay.

BRACHYTHERAPY—A type of radiotherapy in which a small radioactive object is placed inside or next to a tumor to kill cancer cells.

CANCER—A disease in which abnormal cells grow out of control and can spread to other parts of the body.

CATHODE-RAY TUBE—A sealed glass tube in which electrons are fired through a vacuum. It was used in early experiments and in old TV screens.

CHEMOTHERAPY—The use of special medicines to kill or slow the growth of cancer cells.

DECAY—The process by which the nucleus of a radioactive atom breaks down and releases energy.

ELECTROMETER—A device that measures tiny amounts of electric charge or voltage.

ELECTRON—A subatomic particle with a negative charge. It is found in all atoms.

ELEMENT—A substance made up of only one kind of atom. Examples include oxygen, gold, and uranium.

FLUOROSCOPE—A device with a screen that shows X-ray images of the inside of the body in real time.

FOSSIL—The remains or imprint of a plant or animal that lived a long time ago, usually found in rock.

GAMMA RAY—A form of high-energy radiation released from the nucleus of an atom. It can pass through most materials.

HALF-LIFE—The time it takes for half of the atoms in a sample of a radioactive substance to decay.

IONIZATION—The process by which atoms lose or gain electrons and become charged particles called ions.

ISOTOPE—Atoms of the same element that have the same number of protons but different numbers of neutrons.

METALLOID—A substance that has some properties of metals and some of nonmetals.

MOLECULE—A group of atoms bonded together.

NEUTRON—A subatomic particle found in the nucleus of an atom. It has no electric charge.

NUCLEAR ENERGY—The energy released from changes in the nucleus of an atom, especially during fission.

NUCLEAR FISSION—The splitting of the nucleus of an atom, which releases a large amount of energy.

NUCLEAR MEDICINE—A way of diagnosing or treating illness using tiny amounts of radioactive substances inside the body.

NUCLEUS—The central core of an atom, consisting of protons and neutrons.

ONCOLOGY—The branch of medicine that deals with the study and treatment of cancer.

PET SCAN—A type of medical scan that shows how the organs inside the body are working by detecting tiny particles called positrons.

PITCHBLENDE—A dark mineral that contains uranium and was used by the Curies in their discovery of radioactive elements.

PLUM PUDDING MODEL—An early model of the atom in which electrons were thought to be spread through a positively charged cloud, like plums in a pudding.

POSITRON—A tiny particle with the same mass as an electron but with a positive charge.

PROTON—A subatomic particle found in the nucleus of an atom. It has a positive electric charge.

QUADRANT ELECTROMETER—A device that measures electric charge by using a mirror to reflect light onto a ruler.

RADIATION—Energy that comes from a source and travels through space. It can take the form of particles or electromagnetic waves.

RADIOACTIVITY—The release of energy from the nucleus of an unstable atom as it breaks down.

RADIOMETRIC DATING—A method of finding out the age of rocks or fossils by measuring how much of a radioactive isotope has decayed.

RADIOTRACER—A tiny amount of radioactive substance used in medical scans to help doctors see how the body is working.

INDEX